15 Days of Prayer
With Saint Thomas Aquinas

15 DAYS OF PRAYER

WITH

Saint Thomas Aquinas

SUZANNE VRAI AND ANDRÉ PINET

Translated by Victoria Hébert and Denis Sabourin

Liguori
LIGUORI, MISSOURI

Published by Liguori Publications
Liguori, Missouri
http://www.liguori.org

This book is a translation of *Prier 15 Jours Avec Thomas D'Aquin,*
published by Nouvelle Cité, 1991, Montrouge, France.

English Translation Copyright 2000 by Liguori Publications.

Library of Congress Cataloging-in-Publication Data

Vrai, Suzanne.
    [Prier 15 jours avec Thomas d'Aquin. English]
    15 days of prayer with Saint Thomas Aquinas / Suzanne Vrai and
André Pinet ; translated by Victoria Hébert and Denis Sabourin. — 1st
English ed.
        p. cm.
    Includes bibliographical references.
    ISBN 0-7648-0656-4 (pbk.)
    1. Thomas, Aquinas, Saint, 1225?–1274—Meditations. 2. Spiritual
life—Catholic Church. I. Title: Fifteen days of prayer with Saint Thomas Aquinas. II. Pinet, André. III. Title.

BX4700.T6 V7313   2000
269'.6—dc21   00-036847

Printed in the United States of America
04 03 02 01 00   5 4 3 2 1
First English Edition 2000

Table of Contents

How to Use This Book

AN OLD CHINESE PROVERB, or at least what I am able to recall of what is supposed to be an old Chinese proverb, goes something like this: "Even a journey of a thousand miles begins with a single step." When you think about it, the truth of the proverb is obvious. It is impossible to begin any project, let alone a journey, without taking the first step. I think it might also be true, although I cannot recall if another Chinese proverb says it, "that the first step is often the hardest." Or, as someone else once observed, "the distance between a thought and the corresponding action needed to implement the idea takes the most energy." I don't know who shared that perception with me but I am certain it was not an old Chinese master!

With this ancient proverbial wisdom, and the not-so-ancient wisdom of an unknown contemporary sage still fresh, we move from proverbs to presumptions. How do these relate to the task before us?

I am presuming that if you are reading this introduction it is because you are contemplating a journey. My presumption is that you are preparing for a spiritual journey and that you have taken at least some of the first steps necessary to prepare for this journey. I also presume, and please excuse me if I am making too many presumptions, that in your preparation for the spiritual journey you have determined that you need a guide. From deep within the recesses of your deepest self, there was something that called you to consider Thomas Aquinas as a potential companion. If my presumptions are correct, may I congratulate you on this decision? I think you have made a wise choice, a choice that can be confirmed by yet another source of wisdom, the wisdom that comes from practical experience.

Even an informal poll of experienced travelers will reveal a common opinion; it is very difficult to travel alone. Some might observe that it is even foolish. Still others may be even stronger in their opinion and go so far as to insist that it is necessary to have a guide, especially when you are traveling into uncharted waters and into territory that you have not yet experienced. I am of the personal opinion that a traveling companion is welcome under all circumstances. The thought of traveling alone, to some exciting destination without someone to share the journey with does not capture my imagination or channel my enthusiasm. However, with that being noted, what is simply a matter of preference on the normal journey becomes a matter of necessity when a person embarks on a spiritual journey.

The spiritual journey, which can be the most challenging of all journeys, is experienced best with a guide, a companion, or at the very least, a friend in whom you have placed your trust. This observation is not a preference or an opinion but rather an established spiritual necessity. All of the great saints with whom I am familiar had a spiritual director or a confessor who journeyed with them. Admittedly, at times the saint might well have traveled far beyond the experience of their guide and companion but more often than not they would return to their director and reflect on their experience. Understood in this sense, the director and companion provided a valuable contribution and necessary resource.

When I was learning how to pray (a necessity for anyone who desires to be a full-time and public "religious person"), the community of men that I belong to gave me a great gift. Between my second and third year in college, I was given a one-year sabbatical, with all expenses paid and all of my personal needs met. This period of time was called novitiate. I was officially designated as a novice, a beginner in the spiritual journey, and I was assigned a "master," a person who was willing to lead me. In addition to the master, I was provided with every imaginable book and any other resource that I could possibly need. Even with all that I was provided, I did not learn how to pray because of the books and the unlimited resources, rather it was the master, the companion who was the key to the experience.

One day, after about three months of reading, of quiet and solitude, and of practicing all of the methods and descriptions of prayer that were available to me, the master called. "Put away the books, forget the method, and just listen." We went into a room, became quiet, and tried to recall the presence of God, and then, the master simply prayed out loud and permitted me to listen to his prayer. As he prayed, he revealed his hopes, his dreams, his struggles, his successes, and most of all, his relationship with God. I discovered as I listened that his prayer was deeply intimate but most of all it was self-revealing. As I learned about him, I was led through his life experience to the place where God dwells. At that moment I was able to understand a little bit about what I was supposed to do if I really wanted to pray.

The dynamic of what happened when the master called, invited me to listen, and then revealed his innermost self to me as he communicated with God in prayer, was important. It wasn't so much that the master was trying to reveal to me what needed to be said; he was not inviting me to pray with the same words that he used, but rather that he was trying to bring me to that place within myself where prayer becomes possible. That place, a place of intimacy and of self-awareness, was a necessary stop on the journey and it was a place that I needed to be led to. I could not have easily discovered it on my own.

The purpose of the volume that you hold in your hand is to lead you, over a period of fifteen days or, maybe more realistically, fifteen prayer periods, to a place where prayer is possible. If you already have a regular experience and practice of prayer, perhaps this volume can help lead you to a deeper place, a more intimate relationship with the Lord.

It is important to note that the purpose of this book is not to lead you to a better relationship with Thomas Aquinas, your spiritual companion. Although your companion will invite you to share some of their deepest and most intimate thoughts, your companion is doing so only to bring you to that place where God dwells. After all, the true measurement of a companion for the journey is that they bring you to the place where you need to be, and then they step back, out of the picture. A guide who brings you to the desired destination and then sticks around is a very unwelcome guest!

Many times I have found myself attracted to a particular idea or method for accomplishing a task, only to discover that what seemed to be inviting and helpful possessed too many details. All of my energy went to the mastery of the details and I soon lost my enthusiasm. In each instance, the book that seemed so promising ended up on my bookshelf, gathering dust. I can assure you, it is not our intention that this book end up in your bookcase, filled with promise, but unable to deliver.

There are three simple rules that need to be followed in order to use this book with a measure of satisfaction.

Place: It is important that you choose a place for reading that provides the necessary atmosphere for reflection and that does not allow for too many distractions. Whatever place you choose needs to be comfortable, have the necessary lighting, and, finally, have a sense of "welcoming" about it. You need to be able to look forward to the experience of the journey. Don't travel steerage if you know you will be more comfortable in first class and if the choice is realistic for you. On the other hand, if first class is a distraction and you feel more comfortable and more yourself in steerage, then it is in steerage that you belong.

My favorite place is an overstuffed and comfortable chair in my bedroom. There is a light over my shoulder, and the chair reclines if I feel a need to recline. Once in a while, I get lucky and the sun comes through my window and bathes the entire room in light. I have other options and other places that are available to me but this is the place that I prefer.

Time: Choose a time during the day when you are most alert and when you are most receptive to reflection, meditation, and prayer. The time that you choose is an essential component. If you are a morning person, for example, you should choose a time that is in the morning. If you are more alert in the afternoon, choose an afternoon time slot; and if evening is your preference, then by all means choose the evening. Try to avoid "peak" periods in your daily routine when you know that you might be disturbed. The time that you choose needs to be your time and needs to work for you.

It is also important that you choose how much time you will spend with your companion each day. For some it will be possible to set aside enough time in order to read and reflect on all the material that is offered for a given day. For others, it might not be possible to devote one time to the suggested material for the day, so the prayer period may need to be extended for two, three, or even more sessions. It is not important how long it takes you; it is only important that it works for you and that you remain committed to that which is possible.

For myself I have found that fifteen minutes in the early morning, while I am still in my robe and pajamas and before my morning coffee, and even before I prepare myself for the day, is the best time. No one expects to see me or to interact with me because I have not yet "announced" the fact that I am awake or even on the move. However, once someone hears me in the bathroom, then my window of opportunity is gone. It is therefore important to me that I use the time that I have identified when it is available to me.

Freedom: It may seem strange to suggest that freedom is the third necessary ingredient, but I have discovered that it is most important. By freedom I understand a certain "stance toward life," a "permission to be myself and to be gentle and understanding of who I am." I am constantly amazed at how the human person so easily sets himself or herself up for disappointment and perceived failure. We so easily make judgments about ourselves and our actions and our choices, and very often those judgments are negative, and not at all helpful.

For instance, what does it really matter if I have chosen a place and a time, and I have missed both the place and the time for three days in a row? What does it matter if I have chosen, in that twilight time before I am completely awake and still a little sleepy, to roll over and to sleep for fifteen minutes more? Does it mean that I am not serious about the journey, that I really don't want to pray, that I am just fooling myself when I say that my prayer time is important to me? Perhaps, but I prefer to believe that it simply means that I am tired and I just wanted a little more sleep. It doesn't mean anything more than that. However, if I make it mean more than that, then I can become discouraged, frustrated, and put myself into a state where I might more easily give up. "What's the use? I might as well forget all about it."

The same sense of freedom applies to the reading and the praying of this text. If I do not find the introduction to each day helpful, I don't need to read it. If I find the questions for reflection at the end of the appointed day repetitive, then I should choose to close the book and go my own way. Even if I discover that the reflection offered for the day is not the one that I prefer and that the one for the next day seems more inviting, then by all means, go on to the one for the next day.

That's it! If you apply these simple rules to your journey you should receive the maximum benefit and you will soon find yourself at your destination. But be prepared to be surprised. If you have never been on a spiritual journey you should know that the "travel brochures" and the other descriptions that you might have heard are nothing compared to the real thing. There is so much more than you can imagine.

A final prayer of blessing suggests itself:

> Lord, catch me off guard today.
> Surprise me with some moment of beauty
>   or pain
> So that at least for the moment
> I may be startled into seeing that you are
>   here in all your splendor,
> Always and everywhere,
> Barely hidden,
> Beneath,
> Beyond,
> Within this life I breathe.

—Frederick Buechner

REV. THOMAS M. SANTA, CSsR
LIGUORI, MISSOURI
FEAST OF THE PRESENTATION, 1999

A Chronology of the Life of Saint Thomas Aquinas

THOMAS AQUINAS was one of the greatest and most influential theologians of all time as well as being a philosopher and Doctor of the Church (Angelic Doctor). He is the patron saint of Catholic universities, colleges, and schools. His feast day was originally March 7, but was changed in 1970 to January 28.

Although the great outlines and important events of his life are known, his biographers differ as to some of the details and dates. For example, his exact birth date is not known. It is accepted to have been circa 1225, but various sources differ on this, some saying it was at the end of 1226, others attesting to a mid-1227 date for his birth. The majority of sources consulted have noted it to be "circa 1225." All agree that he died on March 7, 1274.

c. 1225: Thomas, the seventh child (and youngest son) of Landulph, the Count of Aquino and Theodora, the Countess of Teano, was born in the family castle in Aquino, a town in southern Italy near Naples. Before his birth, a holy hermit (Fr. Bono) told his mother: "your child will enter the order of Friars Preachers and, so great will be his learning and sanctity that, in his day, no one will be found to equal him."

1232–1243:

At the age of five, according to the custom of the times, he was sent to school with the Benedictine monks at Monte Cassino; yet it is also said that this "customary act" was, in his case, purely a political decision as his uncle was the abbot and Thomas was being groomed to be his successor.

Thomas was noted, at an early age, to be of superior intellect, very devoted to prayer, and meditative, yet he never mastered the art of calligraphy (which may explain his unintelligible writing and the necessity for the use of secretaries). He was often heard asking the question: "What is God?"

In 1236, he was sent to the University of Naples at the insistence of his uncle (the abbot) who felt that a boy of such talents should not "be left in obscurity." He was trained in natural sciences, logic, grammar, and rhetoric as well as music, mathematics, and astronomy.

Thomas was said to have expressed a maturity that was beyond his years; he was a genius and often surpassed his Masters in his knowledge on all subjects. He was pure of heart, resolving to enter the Order at the age of fourteen in spite of his Father's objections.

1244–1247:

This young man of noble birth entered the Order (Dominicans) of poor friars in either 1243 or 1244, much to the surprise of the residents of Naples. His mother, a recent widow, forgetting the hermit's prediction, and very much disturbed by his decision, rushed to the city—the Dominicans, fearing she would take Thomas away, sent him to Rome. During his trip, Thomas's brothers, who were soldiers, captured him and confined him to the fortress of San Giovanni at Rocca Secca. He was detained here for nearly two years as his family members tried, by various means, to destroy his vocation and break down his virtue. It was at this time, after they attempted to destroy his virtue with a temptress, that Thomas knelt in prayer, and asked God to grant him integrity of mind and body. He is reported to have fallen asleep and, during his sleep, two angels appeared to him, assuring him that his prayer had been heard, and mystically fastening him with the white girdle of perpetual virginity. From that day on, Thomas never experienced any further stirrings or temptations. During these two years of captivity, his mother relented and allowed him some reading materials (the Bible, Aristotle's *Metaphysica*, and Lombard's *Sentences*). He was finally set free as the family feared reprisals from the pope. Thomas was returned to the Dominicans who found that Thomas had made as much progress as if he had been in "studium generale"; he immediately professed his vows and was sent to Rome where he studied to be a theologian with, amongst others, Albert the Great, in whose company he went to Paris to the university.

1248–1256:

In 1248, Thomas accompanied Albert to Cologne to found the "studium generale" where he would remain for four years, teaching. He was ordained at the age of twenty-five.

Thomas frequently preached God's word in Germany, France, and Italy during this time.

In 1252, he was sent back to Paris to teach in Albert's place—this is considered to be the beginning of his public career. His duties consisted mainly of explaining Lombard's *Sentences*—his commentaries on this, for the most part, created the material for his major work, *Summa Theologica*.

A conflict between the Church and the University delayed the conferring of the Doctorate on Thomas, but in 1256 orders were sent from the pope that the mendicant friars were to be admitted to the Doctorate.

1257–1272:

On October 23, 1257, Thomas was admitted to the degree of Doctor of Theology along with his friend, (Saint) Bonaventure. From this time onwards, Thomas's life can be summed up in a few words: praying, preaching, teaching, writing, and traveling. His intelligence was known across the land, popes and kings alike wanted him near them and valued his advice. His sole passion, it is written, was an ardent zeal for the explanation and defense of Christian truth. He was offered the archbishopric of Naples in 1265, but begged to be able to refuse it because of his devotion to his sacred task. It was during this time, and some say, as a result of his refusal, that the *Summa Theologica* was begun (said to have been conceived in Rome in 1265 during the time when he was in charge of a "studium").

During this period of his life, it is said that he often was abstracted and in ecstasy. As his life progressed, his ecstacies increased.

During this period, he also wrote his *Summa Contra Gentiles* (1258–1264).

1273 and 1274:

In Naples in 1273, after he had completed his *Treatise on the Eucharist*, three of his friar brothers saw him lifted in ecstacy, and they heard a voice coming from the crucifix on the altar, saying: "You have written well of me, Thomas, what reward will you now have?" Thomas was heard to reply: "Nothing other than You, Lord."

On December 6, 1273, Thomas laid his pen aside after having written the third part of the *Summa Theologica* (left incomplete) and treatises on each of the holy Sacraments, but which were stopped in the midst of his treatment of the sacrament of reconciliation. He would neither write nor dictate any more material. He had experienced an unusually long ecstacy that day during Mass upon which he was heard to have said: "I can do no more...such secrets have been revealed to me that what I have written appears to me to be of little value." Thomas began to prepare for his own death.

Pope Gregory X commanded Thomas to prepare for a General Council to be held May 1, 1274, in Lyons. Thomas tried to obey him, setting out on foot in January of that year, but his strength failed. He collapsed near Terracina, close to the Castle of Maienza, the home of his niece, the Countess Francesca Ceccano, where he was taken. The Cistercian monks of Fossa Nuova requested that he be taken to their monastery. Upon entering, Thomas was heard to say: "This is my resting place forever...I will dwell here and I have chosen it." At the request of the monks, it is believed that Thomas dictated a commentary on the Song of Songs (yet this manuscript has never been discovered).

Near death, extreme unction having been administered, Thomas pronounced the following act of faith: "If, in this world, there be any knowledge of this sacrament stronger than that of faith, I wish now to use it in affirming that I firmly believe and know, as certain, the Jesus Christ, True God and True Man, Son of God and Son of the Virgin Mary, is in this Sacrament.... I receive You, the price of my redemption, for whose love I have watched, studied, and labored. I have preached You and taught You. Never have I said anything against You; if anything was not well said, that is to be attributed to my ignorance...if I have written anything erroneous...I submit to the judgment and correction of the Church, in whose obedience I now pass from this life." Thomas died on March 7, 1274. He was buried at the monastery in Fossa Nuova.

Numerous miracles surrounding his death (healings and cures at his tomb) attest to his holiness and he was canonized by Pope John XXII on July 18, 1323. Saint Pius V proclaimed him a Doctor of the Church in 1567 (calling him "the most brilliant light of the Church"), Leo XIII declared him "the prince and master of all scholastic Doctors" on August 4, 1879, and in 1880 designated him to be the patron of all Catholic universities, academies, colleges, and schools throughout the world. In 1918, Saint Thomas became an institution of the Catholic Church by being mentioned in the Code of Canon Law (See CIC 589.1).

Although Thomas lived less than fifty years, he wrote more than sixty works of various length, most of which at the request of authorities in response to a perceived need. There is some discussion that he did not write all of these works, as most were dictated to secretaries, but his biographers assure us that he could dictate to several scribes at the same time. His works may be classified as philosophical, theological, scriptural, apologetic, and somewhat controversial. His philosophical works are mainly commentaries on Aristotle, and his first important theological works were commentaries on Lombard's four books of *Sentences*. A detailed listing of the entire body of his works would be difficult, but some of the most important include the following titles: *Disputed Questions*; *Free Discussions*; *Intellectual Unity Against the Averroistas*; *Treatise on the Truth of the Catholic Faith, Against Unbelievers*; *Opuscum Against the Greeks*; *Office of the Corpus Christi*; *The Catena Aurea*; *Summa Contra Gentiles*; *Summa Theologica*; *Spiritual Readings*. There are many others.

It has been said that Saint Thomas possessed extraordinary powers of concentration and synthesis. No writer since has surpassed him in his ability to express, in so few words, the truth gathered from so many and varied opinions and sources. His works are remarkable for, amongst other things, their accuracy, brevity, and completeness. Pope Innocent VI stated: "with the exception of the canonical writings, the works of Saint Thomas surpass all others in accuracy of expression and truth of statement." Thomas had declared that he had learned more in prayer and contemplation than from men or books.

It has been said that no one, since the time of Aristotle, has exercised such a powerful influence on the thinking world as Saint Thomas. His life's work may be summarized into two propositions: he established a true relationship between faith and reason and he systemized theology.

Abbreviations Used in This Book

S.T.:   Summa Theologica

S.R.:   Spiritual Readings

C.:   Compendium

Introduction

IT IS A PARADOX that one of the greatest contemplatives of the Middle Ages is read so little; the treasures of his thoughts are too hermetically closed into an arduous language that is no longer our own, but which was compulsory at school. Thomas Aquinas, the Angelic Doctor, who remains solely the companion of the theologians, is once again and much too often ignored by the faithful Christian. Another paradox is that it is through humility that we try to follow in his doctrinal and spiritual ascension.

In the most basic aspect of monotheism, God would be the basis for our prayer just as he was for the *Summa Theologica*: God is our Rock, the solid foundation which, like the desert, lifts the soul by its very own austerity. As Christians, we will not forget that God is first and foremost the Father and it is thus that he asks us to pray. Seek God! Is that not human wisdom? At all times, consciously or unconsciously, man has been searching for something or someone that is greater than he is. Human wisdom leads to divine wisdom, from that which has been created to that which is not, and the heart of man penetrates God's heart, for, through the sending of his Son, God called man first. The Spirit of God comes to meet that of mankind since "the abyss calls to the abyss," according to the Psalmist, and mankind's heart can only take its rest in God.

Mary, the Mother of God and the Mother of the Church, introduces us into the mystery of the Incarnation: she, chosen from all women by God and designated for all eternity, gave a

God to the world that was "conceived of the Holy Spirit and born of the Virgin Mary," not a superman nor a demiurge (the creator of the universe that is subordinate to the supreme being), but a God that united, in his person as the Son, the two clear and distinct natures. Who is this Jesus of Nazareth who allows himself to call God his Father, to personally interpret the Scriptures and make himself God's equal?

Only his death and Resurrection can bring us an answer to these questions: "He is truly the Son of God," or "This Jesus who you have crucified has been arisen from the dead by God." The Resurrection, Ascension, and his sitting at the right hand of the Father and glorification are simply different facets of the same paschal mystery. Whoever may question the real function of these events that happened some 2000 years ago can find an answer through a meditation on the precious blood of Christ, for this blood that was shed on the cross still flows, no longer in the horror of suffering, but in the sacraments of the Church. It is mystical blood in which those who are baptized are plunged, blood that is shed and gathered in the chalice at each Eucharist. The Church, our mother, next to God our Father, introduces us into the mysteries of God and salvation each and every day.

Just like the angels, mankind was created to see God. Was it the foolishness of vanity? No, even the imagination is not foolish enough to reach all the way to reality! Saint Thomas confirms for us that we are not the subject of a pious reverie, but that the plan for salvation is, in a brilliant way, divine. Only the one who is infinite love could conceive of and realize that.

DAY ONE

The Angelic Doctor

FOCUS POINT

Saint Thomas Aquinas was a brilliant man and a prolific writer. But Thomas did not pen a single word before praying on it first. Thomas received the gift of life from God and shared in God's presence through prayer. And it was in prayer that God revealed himself to Thomas. Thomas gained knowledge of God primarily through reason, but also through an infused knowledge that we human beings who are truly blessed experience so briefly in our earthly lives, the vision of God that the angels in heaven know always.

"'What reward will you now have for your work?' asked the Lord. Thomas Aquinas replied: 'Nothing other than You, Lord'" (cited by William of Tocco, Vita).

T homas Aquinas is commonly called the Angelic Doctor yet
he did not have the nature of an angel—a being without
material form and completely spiritual; he was just like us, a being of flesh, who is both spiritual and with a material form. What
was it then that made him worthy of the title "angelic"?

Religious tradition considered monastic life to be an angelic
life. The angels' vocations were their permanent presence next to
God and adoration of Him; (from within) contemplation and
adoration are but one and the same act. With respect to the monks,
it is the same in that their lives must be centered on God through
continuous personal prayers, *lectio divina* and the Divine Office.

In the Sacred Liturgy, temporal prayers unite with the eternal
prayers of the angels. The Divine Office, which is the earthly liturgy of the monks, is united with the heavenly liturgy where heaven
("along with the angels and archangels") and the Earth are united
into one single voice singing: "Holy, holy, holy Lord, God of power
and might, heaven and earth are full of your glory," which we
find in the Sanctus and Te Deum. Mass is continuously being
celebrated around the world through which this perpetual Sanctus
rises to the heavens, bringing a co-penetration of heaven and earth.

Angels have very particular knowledge of God and that was
also true for Thomas Aquinas. It was very certainly his knowledge of God that made him the recipient of the title "angelic."
Pope Innocent IV wrote the following about the life of Thomas:
"To our dear son Thomas Aquinas, a man distinguished by his
noble blood and the brilliance of his virtues, to whom the grace
of God has granted the treasure of the knowledge of the Scriptures" (See Pius XI, Encyclical *Studiorum Ducem*).

The angels, through their nature as pure spirits, "Beings that
are first and supreme among all beings," have a greater knowledge about God than we do. They are more perfect in, and closer
in their resemblance to God. Blessed with the ability to reason
and also having free will, they can choose, right from the time of
their creation, to say to God: either "I will not serve you" or
"may it be done to me according to your will."

"The angel, instantly, after his first act of faith made him merit the blessing, was instantly beatified" (S.T. Ia, Q62:5). Their choice is definitive and without any possible retraction. Their knowledge of God and their nature are such that a simple refusal systematically leads them onto a path of no return. In fact, to see God and to live in his presence, an exceptional place that is given by God to these beings, could leave no room for anything else unless it was nothing short of a rebellion. That is why they either remain good angels—by serving and adoring God—or, to the contrary, through their "no," which is the sin of vanity (stronger with them than with mankind as they are superior beings), they forevermore become demons with no possibility of remission of their sins. It is to be noted here that, at times, in the case of angels, we may find a one-time "exceptional" circumstance, such as, for example, when God lets us know our vocation. We must decide to either answer the call or not! If this call is perfectly evident for some people, for others it is more vague and their search for it is more painful, but there must always be an answer.

The sacraments of marriage or first Communion only happen once even if, in the case of Communion, it will be followed by many others. That is a one-time situation. Saint Thomas, by his inflexible decision to consecrate himself to God, is not without a connection to the angels. May we all have such determination.

We, as humans, can vacillate between yes and no. Our "no" to the divine will could, after reflection, become a "yes" much in the same way as an initial "yes" could change to "no" through outrage, thus, through vanity. The parable of the father and his two sons is a good illustration of this (See Mt 21:28–30). In it, the father asks his sons to go and work in the vineyard; the first replied negatively, then later went and the second said yes and did not go! This reminds us of Jesus' teachings: "May your yes truly be yes!" The son who answered negatively went back on his decision because he came to realize, through reasoning, that he had not chosen the right path and through a movement of repentance, he went back on his decision by finally adhering to the will of the father. That is what is called reconciliation! We can't just give half of ourselves to God, we must give of ourselves totally. To follow Christ is total abandonment: our father, mother, brothers, sisters, and goods; it is a total stripping of one's everything. The commitment is a total one: "'Follow me and I will make you fish for people.' And immediately they left their nets and followed him" (Mk 1:17–18); and "Whoever loves father or mother more than me is not worthy of me; and whoever loves son or daughter more than me is not worthy of me" (Mt 10:37).

We can notice—many other examples are available in the Gospels—that in order to follow Christ, we must make our bodies and spirits completely available to him; he must become the center of our lives. Saint Thomas's "yes" to God, just like that of the angels, knew neither repentance nor regret—that was his holiness.

Saint Thomas of Aquinas' entire life, right from his earliest childhood years, reflected an intense search for God and a total acquiescence to his will. At the age of seventeen, he told his family that he would be a Brother Preacher! He continued to wear the vestments of this order even when they had been torn to shreds by his brothers during his imprisonment. Nothing could ever stop him. Just like the angel, he offered himself to God and to whatever order he wished him to be a part of in a single instant. It was, then, in spirit, that he first gave himself to God; his body would follow—through his studies and again later when he would teach, all the way to his refusal of an honorary position. He only wanted to teach and spread the truth!

One day, later in his life, when Jesus addressed Thomas to ask him what reward he wanted for his work, Thomas answered: "Lord, nothing other than you!" Is that not an example of the action of filial trust, putting aside all of one's personal will in order to give oneself to the One who could only give us what is best for us? Was that a way in which God tested Thomas's humility? The only reward that Thomas wanted was God himself, the best of all rewards. If Thomas had studied, worked, and kept watch, it was in order to always delve deeper into an intimate relationship with God, for the love and through the love of God.

There is a conflict between seeking God throughout one's entire life, which is a human activity, and seeing God "face to face" in an eternal moment, which is an angelic one. When it seems that we have found God, there is a danger in believing that we possess him in his entirety, a complacency in our spiritual life could lead us to distance ourselves from him. That is why the search for God must be a continuous effort which constantly re-news itself, a thirst that can only be quenched by the Source of Living Water. Saint Thomas's life, just like that of the angel, was a "face to face" meeting with God—one through faith, the other in glory. Oh, to be able to see God!

Through the grace of God, he revealed himself to Thomas. Let us remember here that Thomas never wrote a single line of text without having had prior recourse to prayer and contempla-tion. It was then, thus, that Thomas's life was guided by the two wisdoms that he defined as: *"The wisdom that man acquires through study...allows him to have righteous judgment about divine things according to his perfect use of reasoning...but the other wisdom, which is a gift from heaven, judges divine things by virtue of a certain common nature with them. It is a gift from the Holy Spirit...through which mankind is rendered perfect in the order of divine things, not only by learning, but by experienc-ing these things within himself"* (S.T. IIa–IIae, Q45:1, 2, 2a).

Thomas also said, with reference to his knowledge, that "he had received it from God and not acquired it through study or his own work."

In these two quotations, there is a conflict between what man "learns," which man does in a discursive way and through rea-soning, and what he "experiences" through intuitive knowledge (essential for an angel), that is, the perception of a total truth without having recourse to reason. However, we can also have this same type of experience. With the mystics, we call it "enlightenments" or "revelations," whether they are large or small, which come to the spirit without benefit of a sense of reason; but we always come back to the discursive search. Just like the angels, Thomas, more than most humans, benefited from such infused graces.

If the angels' adoration is immediate and perpetual, for man it is different, even if it exists within him as infused knowledge; it passes through different degrees of visions before coming to a beatific vision. God's mercy follows it and man's definitive choice will be the one he will make at the end of his life when he meets God "face to face."

An episode in the Gospel helps us understand what this choice brings to us. The good criminal that was crucified next to Christ realized that his punishment was merited because of his own actions and that Jesus had never done anything wrong. His last words were, first, a recognition of his sins, followed by: "Jesus, remember me when you come into your kingdom" (Lk 23:42). It was a decisive choice for him to turn to God, which brought him this answer from Jesus: "Truly I tell you, today you will be with me in Paradise" (Lk 23:43).

It was important that Jesus said "today" because it could only signify that an act of faith and love towards God, on the eve of our own death, will be immediately followed by his reply of love and the entrance into the kingdom.

Christian friends, naturally, we must "enter into the joy of our Master." May we know him, meet him, and love him with all of our hearts and strength; all of this is, initially, from the standpoint of reason. The experience of God's love and meeting him, beyond the sensory graces received, the spiritual battles won, and triumph over all sorts of trials, gives us proof that the freedom of the children of God rests in one single and unique thing: total self-abandonment to the divine will. In this way, like Thomas, we can also be considered angelic.

REFLECTION QUESTIONS

How have I come to know God in my life? That is, in what ways and in what manner has God revealed himself to me? Do I call upon God's grace for all of my activities, as Thomas did in preparation for his writing? How might God's presence in my daily activities—regardless of how mundane they might seem to be—transform myself and those I come in contact with into graced people involved in a grace moment? Could I make an effort to pray on these daily activities before I embark on my daily routine so that I am aware of God's presence throughout my day?

DAY TWO

About Humility

FOCUS POINT

Humility means totally trusting in God. To trust wholly in one's self is folly, for we are easily distracted, easily misled, weak to temptations. But when we trust in God we stand on solid ground. And when we focus our attention fully on God, when we recognize that he is the source of all our talents, then we become small and he works through us. Our pride is no longer an obstacle to his will. We must focus on God and his divine will; only then will we serve as an ideal conduit for his love.

"Thanks to God, never has my knowledge, my position as a Master, nor any scholarly activity ever given me any movement of vainglory that would lift my soul from the base of humility; and if such a movement would have ever occurred, all that sufficed is only one judgment coming from my sense of reason in order to suppress it" (Thomas Aquinas, as cited by William of Tocco).

God only reveals himself to the little ones and not to those who are wise and intelligent (See Mt 11:25 and Lk 10:21). Yet Thomas was a wise and scholarly man; wise in that he lived guided by the Holy Spirit and scholarly since his intelligence was out of the ordinary. Today, we would call him "gifted"! Certainly, but this intelligence that was given to him through grace was the fruit of his "smallness," his profound humility and his charity, the primary source of all virtues. Furthermore, through constant prayer, as well as long hours of prayer which were bathed in tears, he asked God to grant him the ability to pierce his unfathomable mysteries. If God revealed to him one day: "Thomas, you have written well of me," was it not because he had been totally "humbled under the powerful hand of God" and fully subject to the divine will?

This is what his personal secretary, Reginald de Piperno reported: "Each time he wanted to study, undertake a solemn discussion, teach, write, or dictate, he began by retiring into the secret place of prayer and prayed, shedding tears, so that he might gain knowledge about the divine mysteries. Thanks to this prayer, whenever he had doubts about what he was studying, he prayed, and when he prayed, he came to receive enlightenment. If he had problems before having taken recourse in prayer, he prayed and miraculously found the solution to his problems."

Throughout his life, Thomas never stopped thinking only of God, existing only for God and making his mysteries known. Nicknamed the "silent bull of Sicily," he spoke little when he opened his mouth that did not have God as its subject. Thomas never stopped fighting, at times with great theological masters, so that the truth and only the truth would be revealed. Man can only live by losing himself to this truth.

The Gospel says: "If any of you put a stumbling block before one of these little ones who believe in me, it would be better for you if a great millstone were fastened around your neck and you were drowned in the depth of the sea" (Mt 18:6). That is why Thomas, so gentle and humble, fought constantly. Salvation is for us all, therefore no one could be permitted to teach false doctrines.

It would be paradoxical to speak of humility while lacking some of it or being full of oneself, or for that matter, while giving up. Faced with three masters, Saints Augustine, Benedict, and Anselm, whose ideas he did not totally embrace, Thomas did not resign from his own but, after having demonstrated his own ideas, showed the truth that was expressed by his predecessors.

Following tradition, he admitted that submission to one's superiors, equals, and even to one's inferiors required a growth in humility. Like Saint Augustine, he stated that humility is even more necessary and difficult when one occupies a high-ranking position which plays an important role in society; but he maintained that this virtue dwells in, or flows from, our vision of God. *"Humility, in its specificity, principally concerns the subordination of man to God, because of whom he submits himself to, and also to others when he humbles himself....humility particularly concerns the reverence through which man submits himself to God."*[1]

A former student of Saint Benedict's sons (the Benedictines), Thomas knew the "Rule" and its seventh chapter that spoke about humility. What Benedict had written as a legislator and spiritual master, Thomas wanted to support as a theologian. He kept the twelve degrees by limiting them to being founded on basic principle; *"these degrees must be taken by considering reality itself, that is, the nature of humility"*—that which signifies our relationship with God. Man must always grow and lift himself up but nature hinders this. This urge must be controlled in order to avoid the trap of pride: that is the role of humility. It is more concerned with what is in the heart than what is exterior: *"Humility, like many other virtues, goes from the interior to the exterior. In the degrees that are shown* (inverse order to Saint Benedict), *we are wrong to place what belongs to exterior actions before*

---

[1] All quotations in this chapter are from S.T. IIa–IIae, Q61.

what belongs to interior actions." Thomas then will rediscover and comment on the order followed by Saint Benedict in his twelve degrees of humility: to first place man before God, then before others for *"not only must we revere God in himself, but in everything that is from him, yet not in the same way as we revere God.... We must show adoration for God alone."* He sought support for this from 1 Peter (2:13): "For the Lord's sake accept the authority of every human institution...." Every man represents God since he is created in God's image and likeness.

Both the body and the soul express humility. *"The principle and root of this double behavior is man's reverence to God."* The feeling of God's presence should hold man back in his growth, supervise it, and prevent *"man from judging himself to be better than he is."* Thus, a fear of God and remembering his commandments will form the basis of humility, for if we look at God, we are already judging ourselves to be better than we are and placing ourselves in truth. The first degree of this virtue is a gift from God, from the Holy Spirit. Starting from a reverential fear of God and building upon it, Thomas would construct his scale of humility: thoughts about God moderate our legitimate desire for greatness, help us to appreciate ourselves, and regulate our behavior.

Like a tree lifts itself towards heaven, man and woman must grow, it is a law of nature that is confirmed by the Revelation. To impoverish and diminish oneself comes from a particular vocation, and that is in virtue of spiritual growth in the imitation of Christ who, from a divine condition, stripped himself of everything, taking on our human nature and making himself a slave to it all the way to the cross. If growth is normal and natural, its excess, the foolishness of greatness, comes from pride; from which we must distrust our own will. Saint Benedict wrote that we must not take pleasure in doing our own will and Thomas agreed: the trap of pride that insinuates itself is the desire to build oneself up.

Mistrust in oneself naturally leads to confidence in someone else, in a superior being, God. It is not quitting but remitting. In the same way as the navigator relies on his instruments as he can't do it alone, the Christian, by mistrusting his own tendencies, asks for help. An outlook that is too human would not reach the conclusion of choosing a good spiritual father, man being such a poor judge of himself. Constant faithfulness to his suggestions will be seen: *"To subject oneself with obedience to the superior."*

It is certain that this obedience will meet with difficulties, tough times when there will be temptations to make another choice. At those times, let us remember that the one who perseveres will be saved. Thus, Thomas explained that the humility that is expressed through obedience to a spiritual guide, through the mistrust of ourselves, through recourse to the will of God as expressed by someone else, and faithfulness to this decision even during and especially in the tough times, is: *"To patiently embrace difficult things through obedience."*

Moderation in our desires for greatness, mistrust of ourselves, and trust in God's representative will lead us to descend into ourselves and grant us a better knowledge of ourselves.

The exploration of our own soul, a descent into ourself, and an ascent to God is formidable for it projects the light of truth, which reveals the good from misery. *"To recognize and confess one's own faults"* is the fruit of the divine light, for this recognition of evil within us is already holy. "Know yourself!" Neither Benedict nor Thomas denied these philosophical words; to the contrary, they gave them a more profound and supernatural significance.

This spiritual speleology (exploration in depth) will reveal our inability, unworthiness, and uselessness: *"To believe and avow ourselves to be unworthy of and useless in all things!"* We find ourselves thrown down to the ground, humiliated, but not yet humbled, faltering in our movements, to discover one's nothingness precludes all desire for action. But a virtue always has its opposite, Saint Thomas said, and the effects of humility that are, at times, harmful, are compensated for by those of the magnanimity that show us the greatness of man created in the image of God, who can and must act.

There is only one way to recognize one's nothingness and put ourselves after everything else: *"To believe oneself to be and tell oneself that they are the most untrustworthy of all."* Thomas explains this to us, then the battle between humility and magnanimity: *"Humility suppresses the desire through fear that it tends to greatness by pushing aside reason. Magnanimity pushes the spirit to that which is great by conforming itself to reason. It then appears that magnanimity is the opposite of humility but just the contrary, what they have in common is that they both conform themselves to righteous reason."* When humility and magnanimity have mutually embraced in peace, we have reached a serious stage.

Humility is born in the heart and expresses itself through the body: *"From this humble interior disposition comes certain exterior signs through words, actions, and gestures which manifest what is hidden in the interior...."*

For the monk, obedience is the Rule and mistress of all activities; one must have a general attitude of it that is global. Benedict and Thomas will explain two particular aspects.

Humility must also appear in one's words. Too many people "take the floor," and our two masters would prefer it if *"man did not forestall the moment of speech...that he remain silent until he is asked to speak."* Benedict also speaks of "possessing his silence." Someone who has received the mission to speak must then do it in all humility. *"He only said a few words but they were heartfelt, gentle, without levity, with humility and seriousness, avoiding any raising of the voice."*

Humility expresses itself again through modesty in one's exterior gestures: *"When we suppress, for example, the harshness of our gaze and hold back exterior laughter and other signs of inappropriate happiness...and show ourselves always humble of heart and body by keeping our eyes fixed on the ground."*

Thus, Saint Thomas reiterates the twelve degrees of humility that were presented by Saint Benedict in his Rule. He gave them theological armor that was based on the vision of man before

God and showed that humility that was only apparent was a hypocrisy. True humility of heart must show through one's actions.

Few authors knew, as well as Saint Thomas, to unite humility and magnanimity. The greatness of the *Summa Theologica* came from the smallness of its author and the greatness of the man from his submission to God. Paradoxically, humility makes human greatness for, through it, we situate ourselves in total truth before God. Created in God's image and likeness, we must reestablish it within ourselves.

REFLECTION QUESTIONS

Do I recognize all the gifts I possess as originating from God? Do I find crediting God a difficult task at times, especially when I am praised for my successes by others? How do I maintain a sense of humility and perspective in my daily life? Do I direct the praise I receive to the source of my achievements? Am I focused on God during my good works or when I receive praise? How can I become more centered on God? Can I devote more time to him in prayer? Perhaps a periodic fast would help in this regard.

DAY THREE

God

What words can we use when we speak of God? No words we possess do him justice. No words capture his essence. Once we have said something of God we must immediately qualify our statement and understand the limitations inherent within that statement. Once we recognize that the greatness of God is beyond our understanding, and yet he loves us on a personal level, we can love him at this limited, human platform of understanding. As long as we do not say "God is (this or that)" and leave it that, but rather qualify our "God is..." statements with the understanding that we will never completely capture God's essence with our concepts and words, we can love God the very best that we possibly can.

"Where were you when I laid the foundation of the earth?" (Job 38:4).

R ight from his early childhood, Thomas asked the Benedictine brothers of Monte Cassino: "What is God?" Have we asked ourselves this question? And if that is the case, what answers have we received? God is the creator, the invisible one, the inaccessible one, the immutable one, the transcendent one, etc. These are very overwhelming answers: even if the terms given are justified, we feel excluded from the possibility of a relationship with him. However we could answer, which is also true, but which renders him closer to us: he is the creator, but also the Father and Mother; invisible yet living; inaccessible but revealed through his Son that he sent to us; immutable but pardoning for those who come to him with all of their hearts; his transcendence is only equalled by his merciful love. He is the one who doesn't deceive, in whom we place all of our hope through faith, our rock, according to the concrete and realistic expression of the Psalmist.

"*The first being must, of necessity, exist through action, and not just in potentiality*" (S.T. Ia, Q3:1). At first glance, it is difficult to discern an abyss of theological reflection in this phrase, yet there is one. Descartes said "*cogito ergo sum*—I think, therefore I am," and established the precedence of the being over the action, the necessity of existing in order to be able to act, in brief, the transcendence of the being over the action.

By going back in time, we discover God's celebrated revelation to Moses in the book of Exodus: "I am who I am" (3:14). The mystery of the infinite is so far beyond us that whole books have been written about this single verse. God did not give a course in metaphysics to the prophet and it is futile to search for the historical meaning of the revelation there. Nothing could oppose his investigation in the light of the philosophy of Aristotle, it could reveal one of the possibilities contained in this expression. God defines himself as "the one who is," and Jesus assumed that again in order to indirectly show his divinity, at the risk of being stoned: "...before Abraham was, I am" (Jn 8:58). Descartes showed the precedence of thinking over his own thought and over his action of thinking. At Sinai, God revealed to Moses "who" he was; Jesus let us catch a glimpse of the divine being.

Let us meditate on Jesus' words with the help of those of Saint Thomas. For now, let us set aside the humanity of Jesus and bring back the expression to the Son of God, in his divinity: "I am." To the personal and divine "I" is united the action of being taken in its transcendental purity, no past or future, but only the present, a reality without either antecedents or subsequents: "I am." The expression seems to be somewhat inadequate because of its dualistic format. The one who exists is separated from his action of being. Through various thought processes, we can show that, within us, there is someone who exists, and, on the other hand, an action of being. Another effort would show us that, in God, this duality would not be able to exist, for existence merges with the one who exists, totally, completely, and without any distinction: "I am who I am." The divine nature is, then, a single act of being, in all purity.

The biblical image of God, the rock, is so very remarkable in its justice, for he also is "I am." In living memory, our brothers have always seen it and our descendants will probably know it for many generations. It is notable that Saint Thomas began his *Summa Theologica* by the question: "Does God exist?" by marking the precedence of the subject and of his existence over "this being" who is, that is, his nature. This will be the subject of many questions that will follow. It would be a tautology (saying the same thing twice but with different words) to affirm that the question "Does God exist?" is essential, but it is doubly so. For if God did not exist, our faith is in vain, and if he does exist, our life is with him or should be profoundly affected by him. We do not seek, like Saint Thomas did, to establish proof for the existence of God, proof that will only convince believers, for faith exists beyond knowledge and the best arguments do not give it any meaning, but we will seek to penetrate, a little deeper, into this mystery of "I am who I am" through whom everything exists, and who exists only through himself.

Existence is quite a mysterious thing in itself in its absolute form. Who has more of an existence—a fly or a lion, a man or an angel? Existence ignores quantity and quality. In both cases, one has as much as the other. The terms used in the expression a man is "half dead" or "half alive" are stripped of their meaning. The philosophy of being is totally estranged from this language, just like it is different from the one of contemporary medicine that distinguishes between two or three (or more) types of death. The only distinction in this domain is situated between the being of the creator and that of the creatures, the first having no origin other than himself, the second coming directly from the first.

The expression "having no origin other than himself" invites us to meditate on the unity of God, on the dual meaning of the word, for God is one in himself and one in exclusion of all others. The solitude of God! The infiniteness of the being in the womb of the infiniteness of nonbeing! The one who is in the womb of the one who is not, if we could say it, for how can one be in the womb of one who does not exist? Nothingness remains unimaginable to us. The author of the first verses of Genesis, who was as incapable as we are to speak of the nonbeing, used the word *"tohu-bohu,"* but "disorder" is far from signifying the one who does not exist. It is not good that man should be alone, said God, and he created Eve; but God, himself, always remained the Unique One, the All-Powerful, without equal. The first source of everything could be nothing other than unique. God is also one in himself, without parts or distinctions, an absolute unity. Must we, then, eliminate from our language expressions like "I seek your face, Lord" which imply parts and distinct pieces of God? No, but we must realize that God has no face which can identify him as God. I simply think that God knows me but I have trouble realizing that this knowledge is eternal, with no before or after, and that it is nothing other than God's existence, for in him, to know is to be. God loves me...and it is in an identical way through his action of being. The abyss of his love is nothing other than the knowledge of his existence. If knowledge and love in God are identical to his existence, they are identical and God could not know something or someone without loving them! Everything and everyone that he knows he loves! And God knows everything and everyone!

Saint Thomas said that God is immobile, for *"the principle of all movement must be absolutely immobile"* (C., Part 1, ch. 4). This immobility of God appears to be contrary to our faith in a living God, but that is not true, for there does exist a living immobility: the spinning top, or the Earth (they give us an idea of what it is that may perhaps be vague, but still concrete and real). Its movement is a passage from one state to another, God's movement is the passage from a plenitude of being to another that is always greater through endless growth where no end exceeds another. But we must already rectify this. What we want to say is that, in God, immutability is life. And the love of God is like that. God never stops loving, just as he never began. If, through my baptism, I have become a child of God, for him, for all eternity, I am his child. This baptismal act, occurring in a time that has an earthly connection, plunges its roots into God's atemporal infinity. We can compare God to a whirlwind of being, knowledge, and love…an image that, like all others, has a grain of truth, but also its limitations, for the living immobility of God doesn't know how to show itself. The star-filled sky seems to be somewhat fixed in place—how can the naked eye see the paths of the stars or galaxies which travel at astronomical speeds?—that is an approximate image of mobility in immobility!

For us, as humans who are on the path to perfection, it comes closer to our rhythm. For God, the other is the rhythm of his perfection since it is acquired by him. God is infinitely perfect, for *"all beings are perfect with respect to their actions; all beings are imperfect with respect to their strength, lacking action"* (*Summa Contra Gentiles*, I, XXVIII, 6, p. 136). God is pure action, he is also perfect, all perfection, absolute perfection. He is a living perfection, always more perfect and above all, more perfecting. The distinction in God of a quantitative and qualitative perfection remains in vain. If man could be perfect (or nearly perfect) in a particular thing, God could only be perfect in totality. His plenitude of being is also a plenitude of knowledge, love, perfection, holiness, etc. All human qualities find, in this divine perfection, their model from which they receive their own existence.

At times, philosophy presents the created world like a pyramid with the various realms (animal, vegetable, mineral, human) superimposed...or by lifting itself according to a growing complexity, no matter what it is, the essential that consists of not making God, the most evolved creature, *"the summit of the pyramid."* God is above this pyramid and he transcends from the height that separates the creator from the creation.

The astrophysicist demonstrates the universe's workings as the blowing up of an immense balloon, the galaxies separating, one from each other, in time. At the origin of this, they say there is a "Big Bang" that is analyzed in a stupefying manner but which never brings God, the creator, into this expansion; God transcends all in time and place.

While seeking his destiny or origin, since the two are united, the mystic turns to the Great Universal One, the place beyond all places and the time before all time, and strengthens himself to realize the union or even the fusion of these. This is an approach that is respectable and worthy of praise, but because of the revelation, Christians know that the Omnipotent One is near, that the Eternal One cuts across time, and that his Infinite Existence is only equaled by his love. From the tension between these two poles, which are God's immanence (permanently pervading the universe) and transcendence, surges forth the action of his being, which is pure, eternal, and living.

Saint Thomas explains to us that the unity of God, his simplicity, perfection, infinity, intelligence, and will are defined in a single line in our Profession of Faith: *"I believe in one God, the Father almighty."* In fact, by just saying the word "God," which comes from the Greek word "theos," meaning "to want" or "to consider," we proclaim that he is intelligent, thus intentional. By saying that he is "one," we signify that there is not a multitude of gods. And by underlining that he is "almighty," we say that he is infinite and perfect.

In an era in which the philosophy of the future dominates, where present things are already seen in terms of their long or short term futures, God appears to us like something that "is," a stability amidst movement, a reality in the midst of what is fleeting. I know that I am like a breeze that passes, which will be gone tomorrow, and that is why, with all of the strength of my soul, I put all of my hope in, and I cling to, the rock, the one thing that will always remain the same. I like to repeat, with the Psalmist:

"Be to me a rock of refuge, a strong fortress, to save me, for you are my rock and my fortress" (Ps 71:3).

REFLECTION QUESTIONS

What words do I use in my understanding of God? Do I recognize the inadequacy of these words? Do I see the need to qualify any "God is…" statement I might make with the knowledge that my human understanding and tools of language cannot fully express the reality of God? Despite the immensity of God, do I feel like I have a personal, intimate relationship with my heavenly Father? If not, how might I foster a deeper relationship along these lines?

DAY FOUR

Father

FOCUS POINT

Humankind shares in the divinity of God because Jesus Christ has united the two by his Incarnation. We are the brothers and sisters of Christ now and, like Jesus, we call God our Father. But the Father-Son relationship between God the Father and God the Son is distinct from the Father-child relationship the rest of us share. Though both Father and Son (and Spirit) are truly God, without precedence or priority, they are distinct from each other in Person.

"If my father and mother forsake me, the Lord will take me up"
(Ps 27:10).

The words of family and paternity must be first heard concerning God, and then about the creatures (according to what Saint Paul said in his letter to the Ephesians, 3:14–15), 'For this reason I bow my knees before the Father, from whom every family in heaven and on earth takes its name'" (S.T. Ia, Q33:2, 4). With the grace of God, let us turn to the Father of the Eternal Word, of Jesus Christ and our own Father.

God's paternity, already evident in the Old Testament, blossoms in the New. Jesus prayed to God, whom he called Father-Abba, the word is reported numerous times.

Saint Thomas tells us that a name is what distinguishes us from all other people and he concluded: *what distinguishes others from the person of the Father is his paternity. The proper name for this person, then, is that of Father"* (S.T. Ia, Q33:2 RD). The word evokes a relationship between the first and second Persons of the Holy Trinity in such a way that it constitutes a model that can't be found anywhere else on earth or in heaven except in God, according to the text cited above. It is by looking at God that we discover paternity.

The Father is Father only, and in him, everything is a paternity. His divine nature is put into a relationship with that of the Word: God begetting God and, in the inverse, the Son appears to us like *"the light that was born from the light, true God born of the true God."* Human paternity, which is certainly important, does, however, constitute only a modality of the person, the individual that existed before the fathering. In God, this paternity is for all time, for God is the Father just like he is God. By calling him this, it is the first Person of the Holy Trinity that we are calling, the One who eternally begat the Word, the one who is the origin, more than what is comprised in a God, essentially and globally, even personally. There, we touch on the specificity of Christian prayer.

The direct and eternal relationship that unites the Father to the Word, *"Today, I begat you,"* testifies to the aspect of origin that concerns the Father. Our Eastern Brothers insist on this point.

The Son finds his origin in the Father and the Holy Spirit also takes his own from the Father, whether he originated in the Father through the Son or whether we say that he originated from the two, given that the two form but one single source. The Father, then, is situated at the origin of this mysterious divine movement that is Trinitarian, generational, knowledgeable, and loving.

The begotten Son is of the same divine nature as the Father since he is his perfect image. Saint Thomas concluded: *"If the resemblance is perfect, the filiation* (or the paternity) *is perfect, as much for the Father as for people"* (S.T. IIIa, Q32:3, RD), and he adds that the Son of God perfectly resembles the Father. The divinity that constitutes the Father can be found to be identical in the Son, living, eternal, the perfect image of the Father. Father and Son are of the same divine nature and even co-substantial for, with the Holy Spirit, they together form a single unique God, by subsisting in and through himself in the distinction of the three persons. This differentiation creates an order, but one that is without precedence except of its origin: *"In God there exists an order of Persons according to origin, but without priority"* (S.T. Ia, Q42:3 RD). The mystery verges on a contradiction. The precedence implies an inequality between the Persons that is incompatible with their common divinity.

When God begat the Son, the Person of the Father constituted the original term of this generation, but is the Son his own work or that of the three divine Persons? Saint Thomas comes back to the power of generation to the divine nature: *"Paternity is not something by which the Father begets, but that which constitutes the Person of the Father...that by which the Father begets is the divine nature in which the Son totally resembles him"* (S.T. Ia, Q41:5 RD). This confirms for us the "original" aspect that the word "Father" implies. This eternal generation appears like a flash, always active and living, from the divine nature in its plenitude, spreading from the paternity of one to the filiation of the other by making one the origin and the other the ending, Father and Son.

"Abba, Father, for you all things are possible..." (Mk 14:36).

Jesus prayed like this often. Who is my Father? Did Jesus ask this question? Before speaking about this in more detail, let us simply try to enter into the mystery of Jesus and his Father.

The expression "Abba-Father" aims at God, a personal God or at least one that is personified, and the Christian could not escape from the question: Did Jesus address God or the first Person in the Holy Trinity? The question shows a union of person to person between Jesus and his Father. Who are these Persons questioning and being questioned? Are we close to the first notion of paternity that we have just seen? The Son has become incarnate, his words assume a human language that stretches between time and space. If to an eternal and divine "Today, I begat you," could come a divine and eternal response, "Abba-Father," the one that we now see assumes human and temporal form, but substantially and fundamentally, it is the same Abba-Father. The child at the age of twelve or the Rabbi of thirty are one and the same person. In him, body and soul, constitute a perfect human nature which the Word of God assumed: "The Word was made flesh." His Father remains the first Person of the Holy Trinity and he is the second, without either subordination or difference, if it does not come from the origin.

Jesus was born to Mary through the operation of the Holy Spirit (See Lk 1:26–38). Mary is called his Mother with even more precision than Jesus is called her Son, explains Saint Thomas, for in the first case, we apply a human qualifier (his mother) to a human person (Mary) while in the second, we apply a human qualifier (son) to a divine person (the Word). In the relationship between Jesus and his Father, the two qualities of father and son are addressed to the two divine Persons and this relationship, itself, is divine. Jesus has no father in the flesh. Mary was conceived of the Holy Spirit but did not yield to the temptation of seeing him as a carnal father of Jesus. Let us not project our human conceptions on the mystery of Jesus! The Holy Spirit is not Jesus' father either in his divinity, or in his humanity. *"In Christ's conception, the Holy Spirit cannot be called Father"* (III *Sentences*

IV:2, 1, 4). If the Virgin played a passive role and the Holy Spirit an active one, the latter was according to the divine mode. Its efficiency comes back to the entire Holy Trinity: Father, Son, and Holy Spirit. While the origin is properly brought back to the Father, its efficiency is attributed, by appropriation, to the Holy Spirit. Through Luke's words, "The Holy Spirit will come upon you, and the power of the Most High will overshadow you" (Lk 1:35), Saint Thomas discerns the divine nature that is common to the three Persons, designated here by the "power of the Most High" and the Person of the Holy Spirit, efficient by appropriation of the generation without being the origin of it (the Father). Saint Thomas wrote: *"The formation of the body of Christ is attributed to the Holy Spirit"* (C., I, 219), and the word "attributed" signifies the appropriation. To the Holy Spirit is appropriated all works that are done by the Trinitarian God, through the common divine power, but which assumes a character of creation or of re-creation or sanctification. The phrase *"The flesh of the Word of God must have been formed by the Holy Spirit of the Word"* (Ibid) does not negate that the Father remains at the origin of this filiation, that the three Persons were all involved in it and that the Holy Spirit was the one to whom we appropriate this generation.

No person could ever utter the words "Abba-Father" like Jesus, for that expression could not find this same meaning in any human. Through his nature, only Jesus is truly the Son of God and we are his children through his grace. In him, only God speaks to God, that is why if we want to call God our Father, in all truth, we must unite ourselves to him, become one with him. Always, by praying in us, the Holy Spirit puts the actions and feelings of Jesus onto our lips and into our hearts.

Our prayers must begin with the invocation "Our Father"— Christ demanded this of us. By doing this, we follow the precept of Saint Paul: "be imitators of God" (Eph 5:1). Let us imitate Jesus in his prayer "Abba-Father." The thoughts in our prayers, according to the flesh, could orient our hearts towards God, our

Father, by a greater, ever-increasing passage to the reaching of
human limitations. Our trust in God makes us ignore the limitations that are inherent to the flesh. God's teachings makes us more
than just a person, a child of God; our filial love finally ignores
the deficiencies of all fathers of the flesh. The initial "Our Father" demanded by Jesus defines the prayer of a Christian and
differentiates it from his own. Not being him, we can't pray with
his exact terms. The relationship between Jesus and his Father is
a unique one, ours only resembles it. In the same way, Jesus' prayer
comes from a divine Person, who has incarnated into our human
world, and goes to another divine Person. Ours goes from a human to God. But there is only a remote analogy between these
two prayers, the assumption of a human nature by the Word of
God puts the Christian next to the Son and confers on him a
value that comes close to that of the Son. Through the Incarnation of the Eternal Word, his Father became the Father of Jesus,
God and man, and also the Father, the source of all good for
whoever is united, in one way or another, to his Son.

Engendered in his Son through baptism, nourished by the
blood and the flesh of his Son, we participate in the nature of one
and the other. The Father can be called "Our Father" since we
share, by participation, the same nature as he. Again, the power
of the regeneration must be brought back to the omnipotence
that is common to the three divine Persons. Adoption-filiation is
realized by the three, attributed to the Holy Spirit but, at its end,
constitutes children of the Father, in the Son. Perhaps we have
remained, for too long a time, at the threshold of this whirlwind
of love that is the Holy Trinity, as God was nothing more than
the Almighty for us. But today, Christ has seized us: "I came from
the Father and have come into the world; again, I am leaving the
world and am going to the Father" (Jn 16:38), and he says to us:
"I am ascending to my Father and your Father, to my God and
your God" (Jn 20:17).

The Our Father is essentially a communal prayer, for the Word
of God, by taking on a human nature through Mary, draws all

people to him, uniting them together as members of one body that are united to the head, forming one single entity.

There we can also discern the sign of mutual Christian cooperation and that of the charity that unites them in this way as a fulfillment of what Jesus Christ demanded of us: "For where two or three are gathered in my name, I am there among them" (Mt 18:20). Strengthened by this promise, with Jesus and in him, turned to God, we can say:

Our Father, who art in heaven,
Hallowed be Thy name;
Thy kingdom come;
Thy will be done
On earth as it is in heaven.
Give us this day
Our daily bread;
And forgive us our trespasses
As we forgive
Those who trespass against us.
And lead us not into temptation,
But deliver us from evil. Amen.

REFLECTION QUESTIONS

When I pray, do I regard my conversation with God as an intimate, personal encounter? Do I pray to Jesus as if I was conversing with a brother? Do I pray to God the Father, thinking of him in a paternal light? How does this mind-set aid me in my prayer life? Do I ever find that this way of praying sometimes prevents me from perceiving God with a sense of awe? If so, how can I regain a balance in this regard?

DAY FIVE

From Created Wisdom...

FOCUS POINT

True wisdom comes from the divine source, God. Human knowledge is flawed by ignorance and sin. Human perception left unaided is distorted and misleading; it cannot be relied upon for true judgment. God's assistance is needed. He is the source of true wisdom, and when we call upon him in prayer, and when his divine wisdom shines down upon us, we are graced with a glimpse of his divine will. Alone we are in darkness, but with God as our guide we are never lost.

"Therefore I prayed, and understanding was given to me; I called on God, and the spirit of wisdom came to me" (Wis 7:7).

   "Give your servant therefore an understanding mind to govern your people, able to discern between good and evil; for who can govern this your great people?... God said to him,...'because you have asked for yourself understanding to discern what is right,

I now do according to your word. Indeed I give you a wise and discerning mind; no one like you has been before you and no one like you shall arise after you'" (1 Kings 3:9–12).

H ow pleased we are to put this prayer of Solomon, king of Israel, on the lips and in the heart of Saint Thomas! Both of them were great philosophers, friends of Wisdom; a similar request followed by a similar divine reply, but what a difference in its usage! Saint Thomas explicitly proclaimed such a prayer. To be able to acquire Wisdom! Is it not the goal in life for every intelligent being: to become one of those "wise elders," known for their wisdom throughout all lands and by all people? Some people speak all the time, others prefer to listen to the wise elders who seriously explain themselves in a profound manner and, if that would be possible, listen to God himself.

Saint Thomas distinguished two kinds of listening: *"the language of man that speaks around us and God who speaks to us interiorly"* (S.T. IIa–IIae, Q5:1, 3). For opposite reasons, these two kinds of listening seem difficult for people who speak too much and superficially, while God doesn't express himself enough and too profoundly. The acquisition of Wisdom is subject to these difficulties.

Saint Thomas said: *"There are two types of Wisdom: created and uncreated; both are given to man, and by this gift of Wisdom, man can grow towards Holiness"* (De Veritate 11:1, 10). Provisionally, let us assume that uncreated wisdom depends on the other whose acquisition is possible for us since *"both are given to man."* The phrase "are given" is ambiguous. Saint Thomas brought up many means to acquire created wisdom: through our own efforts and as a freely-given gift from God. If the desire to love God is already love, according to Saint Augustine, the desire for wisdom must also be a beginning of wisdom, and we should give thanks to God for this gift. This is not necessarily the desire of all people, nor is it a simple natural proclivity, but a personal vocation that belongs to us. Perhaps others feel this desire; they probably do, but this is personal and intimate. Before one works to gain possession of it, we are easily discouraged if we are not firm in our hope and certainty that God gives what he makes us want. There are many types of wisdom, each has its own particular value and each is desirable, but a general type of wisdom that surpasses and encompasses all others is what draws us. Each has his own wisdom, but we must each aspire to what Saint Paul says: "Strive for the greater gifts" (1 Cor 12:31): knowledge of God, theology, or discussions "about" or "of" God. Human discussions about God are difficult to grasp, their exegeses (criticisms of Scripture) are uncertain and the hermeneutics (interpretations of Scripture) are very subjective. By believing in a teaching that was given by God to man, we turn towards him and draw the desired wisdom from there: *In fact, in its own way, sacred doctrine treats God as the highest origin for everything, that is, already revealed by the entirety of all creation but above all, in a way in which he recognizes himself and in which he is made known to us* (S.T. Ia, Q1:6 RD).

Who are we to think that God speaks to us? First, we must put ourselves into the school of humanity, for it is there that God spoke; this assembly, this *"Ecclesia,"* will be the setting of our search.

God, what do you say about yourself? His reply, transmitted exteriorly by the Church remains insufficient unless it is accompanied by an interior one. The human institution and divine inspiration combine, harnessed to the same yoke, that of a comprehension of the Word of God. One gives us the other, the latter clarifies the former. The external teachings of the Church and the interior teachings of the Holy Spirit complete each other.

The Church proclaims the Word of the Lord in different ways, sometimes about the purity of its origins (the Bible), with its human authors who were inspired by the one, single, unique Author, and sometimes through the pioneers of the Church or Fathers of the Church, finally, by those who, throughout the centuries, have dedicated themselves to study and prayer and have perceived its most profound meaning (like Saint Thomas), whom we call the Doctors of the Church. None of that is essential to salvation, one single interior word could perhaps be of more value than many readings. As long as the latter are not just forums for personal vanity, they could lead to useful interior discussions. Hence, let us regularly ask ourselves about how we listen to the Word, and about how often we read the writings of the holy Catholic Fathers.

What can we say about the amount and variety of kinds of human knowledge? But there is one in amongst all of these that surpasses them all: *"In an absolute manner, we call someone 'wise' who absolutely knows the highest reason, someone who knows God. That is why the knowledge of divine things is called wisdom. On the other hand, that of human realities is called knowledge..."* (S.T. IIa–IIae, Q9:2 RD). Wisdom and knowledge are opposites here, just like one is the opposite of many, or the knowledge of the creator versus that of the creation, but it is only an approximation for the whole world seen in God's thoughts that is the subject of Wisdom. It is enough to just lift up our glance, judge things with respect to God and in relationship to him. The science of astrophysics infinitely enlarges our field of observation of the universe, but the wise man sees God working there. There exists as many kinds of wisdom as there are kinds of knowledge and they proliferate, and in each there are dominant wisdoms, but above them all, the Wise One reigns: *"the one then who is, purely and simply, the supreme origin of everything in the universe, that is, God"* (S.T. Ia, Q1:6 RD).

The situation in time and space of the original Big Bang, its meticulous description that is given on a minute by minute basis is amazing, but it encounters the unbreeched barrier of the beyond by closing the door to all knowledge about the Author of this universe and his motivation. However, it is there that true Wisdom dwells: the knowledge of the "beyond" of our universe and its inaccessible precedence.

That goes beyond our human limitations, but God comes to our aid. Only he knows himself and can speak about himself. If one can acquire Wisdom, it is primarily given, like a gift. Much of human knowledge comes as a result of hard work, but beyond that, there is the gift of God.

At the beginning of our reflection, we affirmed that Saint Thomas prayed in order to obtain Wisdom. He prayed to God constantly, before each theological "disputatio" or important writing. But since a particular prayer to ask for Wisdom has been sent to us, we meditate on it with the regret, which is always compensated, that we have to break it up.

A prayer from an Angelic Doctor could only be developed, and we discern, after an introduction, two identical cycles, followed by a synthesis. *"Ineffable Creator, whose treasures of Wisdom have created three hierarchies of angels and have established them in an admirable order above heaven and who have placed, with such goodness, the parts of the universe...."*[2]

With Saint Thomas, let us address ourselves first to God, to the Creator and, without distinction, to people. In a search for Wisdom, our glance is stopped on the communal Wisdom of the Father, Son, and Holy Spirit which is indistinct, the dispenser of wisdom in the universe. The mention of the three hierarchies of angels, an obvious reference to the nine choirs of angels, does not surprise anyone familiar with Saint Thomas. The angels illuminate each other according to the descending order of the hierarchy: those who are situated higher, closer to God, and filled with an infused knowledge of God and things, illuminate and teach their inferiors. Without expressing it, the Angelic Doctor humbly takes his place behind the smallest of the angels by remembering that they constantly see the face of God. At once, Thomas chose and preferred the Wisdom that was received from above over that, elaborated at great effort, from here below. The Wisdom of God is read in the universe, said Saint Paul, repeating what was written in the Book of Wisdom. Thomas knew it and

---

[2] This text and those which follow in this chapter are translations from citations in *"The Angelic Doctor"* by J. Maritain (DDB, 1930).

showed it, but it was to another Wisdom, even higher still, that he aspired.

"You who are called the True Source and the super- distinguished Principle of the Light and Wisdom, deem to send a ray of your clarity onto the shadows of my intelligence, by removing from me the double obscurity in which I was born, the one of sin and the one of ignorance." This first demand of Wisdom puts the divine Light, which is giving and merciful, in opposition to the shadows of humanity and sin. If the prayer again addresses itself to God, we however perceive a reference there to the Persons of the Father and the Son, of the Father by engendering the Son, the first having been invoked as the Source and Principle, the other as Light and Wisdom. In the request, the contrast is shocking—the Light born of the Light sent into the obscurity of humanity and sin: the normal continuation of the Incarnation of the one whose coming enlightened all people in this world. The obscurity of sin thickens the shadows of ignorance, affirmed Saint Thomas, and the sinner sees his intelligence obscured. Here, Thomas confesses human poverty: his and ours.

"You who have made the language of the small children eloquent, change my speech and pour on my lips the grace of your blessing." This second cycle of questioning and requests, in its brevity, refers first to Psalm 8:3, which can be called upon by the previous mention of angels, and then it refers to the prayer of the deacon's blessing in the preparation of the Eucharist, to the song of the Gospel, by eliciting the blessing of the priest for his heart and his lips. Finally, the expression "change my speech" situates Saint Thomas amongst the great "stuttering" prophets, Moses or Jeremiah, who rightfully lamented about not knowing how to proclaim the Word of God.

"Give me the ability to understand, the capacity to retain, the manner and facility to study, the subtlety to interpret, and abundant grace to speak." These five requests synthesize Thomas's thinking; three concern the superior faculties: the reception of the divine light through intelligence, its retention through memory,

and its diffusion through will; the two others refer to work. Like the above, it is with reference to his own vocation to teach the Word of God that Thomas directed these demands, like Solomon did to govern God's people.

"*Dispose the beginning, direct the advance, fulfill the completion. You who are the true God and true man, and who lives and reigns throughout all the centuries, Amen.*" Finally, Thomas addressed himself to Christ, "the alpha and the omega," the beginning and the end of all things. He knew that God took the initiative; it was not he, Thomas, who decided to write about God, but God who predestined him to do it for all eternity, who led him to it in spite of his family's opposition against the Brothers and who made him reach the pulpit of theology. Our times provide us with an overabundance of information, but there is one choice: may we know, like Saint Thomas and many others, to seek the true Wisdom which comes from above, with the assistance of human wisdom which is already enlightened by grace. Here, Thomas admits that throughout his entire life, divine grace has protected him, guided him, and strengthened him. He gives thanks for this through the Word of Glory:

> *Wisdom is a burning sun*
> *Which it spreads.*
> *Like a sun that is enflamed through the love*
> *That it lights.*

REFLECTION QUESTIONS

In what ways do I attempt to gain wisdom, knowledge of God? Do I engage in regular spiritual reading? Do I read the Catechism on a continuing basis? Participate in a Bible-study program at my parish? Do I pray for God's wisdom to enter my life during these times? Do I understand the importance of God's grace and my need for that grace in regard to my coming to know the Lord through sacred Scripture or Church teaching?

DAY SIX

To Uncreated Wisdom

FOCUS POINT

Jesus Christ, the God-Man, is the combination of uncreated and created wisdom. As God, he is Wisdom, but as a man, he must grow in wisdom by humbling himself before his heavenly Father. In this manner, he is the model of true created, human wisdom. He shows the way to wisdom through his humility, that is, recognizing the limitations of created wisdom, and bowing before the power of uncreated wisdom, that of God. By his Incarnation, uncreated and created wisdom are united, and mankind is gifted with the grace to glimpse God's wisdom in prayer.

"Come to the source of Wisdom,
Come, let us adore God" (Antiphony).

As a result of one's reflections, assisted by the grace and gift of God, created Wisdom finds its uncreated model in God and especially in the Man-God. In Jesus Christ, who was perfectly human and totally God, they both unite. Paradoxically, in him, wisdom grows when he, himself, is Wisdom. From simple to the greatest Wisdom of the elders, the spectrum is wide open: the biblical books of Proverbs and Wisdom give witness to it, by showing us prosaic resourcefulness in professions, occupations, or family conduct and the (divine) Wisdom by presiding over the destiny of the universe. God is Wisdom!

Wisdom is first and foremost an attribute of God: God is wise just as he is eternal, loving, good, and merciful—and his wisdom, like his eternity and goodness, is uncreated, knowing neither time nor place, existing in the timelessness of God. It knows neither growth nor reduction, in the most absolute meaning of the term, it *is*.

Unincarnated Wisdom, you arise from the profound nature of God and are situated beyond the multiplicity of the divine Persons, in the unity of their common being. There is neither a Sage by conceiving nor conceived Wisdom, but the singular Wisdom of an eternal God. Saint Thomas wrote, *"In God, perfections preexist in unity and simplicity"* (S.T. Ia, Q13:4 RD), by it, establishing divine Wisdom as one of God's attributes. We are at the heart of the abyss of God's existence. Only an analogy can help us to get a glimpse of the mystery: *"If we describe a man as 'wise,' it signifies a perfection in him that is distinct from his essence, yet when we attribute it to God, it signifies nothing other than the divine nature"* (S.T. Ia, Q13:5 RD). A man either is or isn't wise; this virtue being distinct from him and secondary, while God could be nothing but wise, for it is part of his essence, his profound divine nature.

While Christ was called "Wisdom" or "the Wisdom of God" at times, were we wrong? Is that outside of the Christian faith? It is neither: quite often, the Church attributed Wisdom to the Word of God. All that comes from the divine nature is indistinctively credited to the three holy Persons and, globally, to God. On the other hand, only the Father could beget, only the Son is begotten, and the Holy Spirit of love comes from both. This particularity to each of the divine Persons gives us the authority to "attribute," to one or another, anything in the strictest sense of the term, that comes from their common nature, first, but which, under a secondary aspect, is not without reminding us of the specific action of one or another of the Persons. Thus, at times, we attribute divine omnipotence to the Almighty Father because he is the "origin" of everything, or all that concerns love is attributed to the Holy Spirit because of his place in the Holy Trinity. In the same way, Wisdom is, at times, attributed to the Son through an analogy with eternal generation: the Father conceived Wisdom like he eternally conceives the Son...from which the Son will be Wisdom.

By calling the Son "Wisdom," it leads us to call the Father "the Wise One" of the Holy Trinity. The expression is never used: God is Wisdom and uncreated Wisdom belongs to the Father like it belongs to either the Son or the Holy Spirit, for they are all God equally. Saint Thomas spoke of a "sapiens" Father like he spoke of the Father by begetting the Word, but much less, by finding a certain resemblance between the generation of the Son by the Father and the wise conception of Wisdom by a Wise One. But he did it more in order to attribute Wisdom to the Word than to attribute the origin to the Father.

If the Father isn't, or is very rarely, called "the Wise One," the Son is more frequently called "Wisdom": *"For various reasons, just like the gift of Wisdom is attributed to the Holy Spirit who is a Gift, in fact, the principle is that all gifts are (expressions of) love; but the same gift of Wisdom is attributed to the Son who is Wisdom...in the same way that the idea that memory is attributed to the Father comes from intelligence"* (De Veritate 7, 3:3). The Angelic Doctor only saw the gift of Wisdom here; this, like other gifts, is attributed to the Holy Spirit. On the other hand, Wisdom is attributed to the Son. The Word of God seems to us to be the Wisdom of the Father. He is first the Son and that is his own name, but just as the word "Son" defines a relationship of generation and the term "Wisdom," one of knowledge, a certain affinity exists between the two, especially if we consider the fact that the first relationship, that of generation, is taken in a purely spiritual sense. The Son is called "the Wisdom of the Father" primarily because he is his Son who was conceived through an eternal generation: "Today, I begat you," and then because this generation is not without resemblance to the intellectual generation that results in Wisdom.

"Just like the Father is a God who begets, the Son-God begotten, in the same way, we must say that the Father is wise (or even better, he accomplishes Wisdom) by conceiving, and the Son is wise (or is a result of wisdom) in as much as he is conceived. In fact, the Son, in as much as he is the Word, is a certain conception of a Wise One. But like all that dwells in God is God, this conception of a Wise God is itself God" (De Potentia 9, 9:6).

It would be tempting to make the Wisdom of the Son totally and directly dependent upon that of the Father, but it is not. Wisdom is not an interpersonal relationship, but a divine attribute.

The Wisdom of God is the infinite Wisdom of the divine nature, a Wisdom that is born of the Father for all eternity. Jesus, in the mystery of his Incarnation, must "grow in wisdom." Starting from zero, that is one aspect of Christ's kenosis with God's humility. By coming onto the earth, O divine Wisdom, you abandoned nothing but, in your new human nature, you must learn everything again. Divine Wisdom, you unite yourself with human wisdom. Immobile in your bounty, you grow in our world.

"The soul of Christ first knew all that, with respect to man, was possible for him to know of his own strengths, but he received the other things from God through revelation, infused knowledge or as a gift of the Holy Spirit, in particular that of Wisdom. This infused knowledge would be much more abundant in the soul of Christ than in all others" (S.T. IIIa, Q11:1 RD). It is impossible to confuse divine Wisdom that you *are* with

the created wisdom that, as a man, you *receive*. To speak of your infused knowledge is to enter into a mystery. The Gospel reports that, as a child, you amazed the Doctors of the Law. Saint Thomas wrote that: *"Christ's infused knowledge was greater and more excellent than that of the angels, as much for the amount of knowledge as for their certainty, Christ enjoys a spiritual light that is much superior to that of the angels"* (S.T. IIIa, Q11:4 RD).

Should we make Jesus out to be a super Saint Augustine or Thomas Aquinas, but who has never written anything? Often a source of pride for man, the knowledge that came from Jesus would have inspired him, to the contrary, to great humility: that is, by saying only what is necessary but knowing much more. Jesus, uncreated Wisdom, your human soul was filled with all of the created Wisdom in concordance to your redemptive mission. Just as, through the Incarnation, God spoke, grew, suffered, and died, in the same way and for the same reason, Wisdom grew and developed in Christ's humanity (See S.T. IIIa, Q16:5). Divine Wisdom was incarnated and the human found himself to have been deified (See Ibid Q16:2).

Willingly, we will identify the meeting of the two Wisdoms with the birth of Christ, but is that not an undue simplification of the question? The "sacred doctrine" that we can also call "the Word of God" is a kind of knowledge, a Wisdom of the highest order. *"The sacred doctrine is at least called 'Wisdom'…because, particularly, it speaks of God, who is the first origin of everything, not only as it is possible to know him through his creation, but also as someone who is impossible to know, known to himself alone, and revealing himself to the world"* (S.T. Ia, Q1:6 RD).

Since Abraham, and perhaps even before, uncreated Wisdom and human Wisdom advanced, one towards the other, to a meeting point, progressing together through the centuries in order to embrace each other definitively in the Person of Christ, the divine Person who lives for all eternity and yet was born of Mary in human time.

The Litany of the Blessed Virgin Mary call this the "throne of

Wisdom." Seated herself on a throne, Mary forms a throne for Jesus out of her knees: the throne of Wisdom. The icon with this name represents a double relationship, or two aspects of a unique reality. Mary constitutes a throne for the Word of God for which we attribute the name of Wisdom; she then presents the Son of God to us. Or, Mary is considered to be the throne of Wisdom, this latter is taken in its strictest sense, it shows then, to the world, the Wisdom of a singular and Trinitarian God, an attribute of God, one of his many aspects, his Wisdom.

With Mary, the earth gave its fruit through the Holy Spirit; God, our God, blesses us in her; human wisdom and God's wisdom embrace each other.

REFLECTION QUESTIONS

In what ways do I humble myself for the sake of growing in wisdom? Do I approach prayer with an open mind and heart, ready to accept all that God graces me to know? Or are their times when my assumptions and those beliefs I hold onto so strongly prevent me from knowing God as well as I might? What methods of prayers, what spiritual acts, might benefit me by fostering a deeper sense of humility within me, pervading my prayer life to the point where I can approach God with a humility that is entirely open to his will and wisdom?

DAY SEVEN

The Holy Spirit, God's Fire

FOCUS POINT

The Holy Spirit is identified with so much: Creation of the world, purification of sins, transformation from fear to courage. The Holy Spirit is prefigured in the Old Testament writings and revealed to humanity by Jesus Christ. The Spirit is the great love between the Father and the Son. In our understanding of God and his Word, the Holy Spirit illuminates the Truth so that we might see and know God's goodness.

"Spirit of love, Maranatha, Spirit of fire, Spirit of God."
"Veni Creator Spiritus—Come, Holy Spirit...
You who are called Paraclete (defender)
Living source, Fire, Charity..." (Hymn for the Pentecost).

L ord, you are a devouring fire and, particularly in you, the Holy Spirit. By commenting on the Book of Isaiah (10:17), Saint Thomas developed this idea: "The light of Israel will become a fire, and his Holy One a flame." The mystery of the fire will lead man to meditation.

"In the expression, 'the light of Israel will become a fire' note that our God is called Fire first because he is held by his substance which is a spirit...through knowledge because he is penetrating...by his invisibility, a hidden God. He is also called Fire because he is shining, he manifests himself to the intelligence and fulfills our love...and directs our actions. In the third case, like fire, God warms us with a life-giving warmth...which also purifies—and at times, destroys.... Finally, this fire is gentle. It leads us according to his mercy to where he is...in love" (See Isa 10).

The lightness of the flame, its subtlety or spirituality make a living symbol for God. God in his being, or his deity, is elusive like a flame, for "God is spirit" (Jn 4:24), and the spirit is ethereal. Without being strict about the term "ethereal," fire evokes immateriality. Just like the angels, God is placed, by the theologian, the painter, or the iconograph, under the sign of fire. Amongst the four elements of our world, fire is the best to evoke the being of another world.

The Word of God penetrates our hearts and souls like fire does and warms our bodies. The author of the letter to the Hebrews wrote: "Indeed, the word of God is living and active, sharper than any two-edged sword, piercing until it divides soul from spirit" (Heb 4:12). We cannot listen to the Word or contemplate it without the slow and deep penetration of it into us—"sharper than any two-edged sword"—and a devouring fire: through the Fire of the Holy Spirit, the Word of the Father, brought by the Son, penetrates, wounds, impregnates the soul and burns it. In the Holy Spirit, this Word takes on its full effectiveness. "The letter kills, the spirit gives life," even the letter of the Word of God, his Gospel, remains in vain without the fire of the Holy Spirit which gives it life.

"God, no one ever saw him"; the spiritual world escapes our senses, and, as a result, also the One who is the source for it all. God remains invisible and Job asked: "But where shall wisdom be found? And where is the place of understanding?" (Job 28:12). In his questions to God, Job did not use the unpronounceable name of the Lord, but one of God's attributes: Wisdom, and a gift of the Holy Spirit, intelligence. "It (Wisdom) is hidden from the eyes of all living" (Job 28:21). Does the revelation put an end to this obscurity? Faith remains half-obscured by bringing a true and authentic light to God but it also deepens the shadows that surround it. That is the Christian paradox. God never appears but, at times, takes on a visible form, in particular, that of fire. In the burning bush, he spoke to Moses, that episode remains a part of both Christian and Jewish traditions, discerning the Word of God there, the presence of the Son, and the fire of the Holy Spirit, even showing a prefiguration of the Holy Trinity. God is a consuming fire, especially the Holy Spirit. Come Spirit of fire, Spirit of God!

A source of light, fire sheds light on and renders things visible. The Psalmist said: "...in your light, we see light" (Ps 36:9). For him, to live near God, in his court, is to rejoice in his divine light; the face of God enlightens our life, transforms it, and gives it meaning. The light of the Holy Spirit manifests the mystery of God in us, enlightens it, and leads our search. Four gifts from the Holy Spirit—wisdom, intelligence, knowledge, and advice—open us to knowledge of God and help us to penetrate his mystery. The gift of Wisdom, the greatest gift—according to Saint Thomas— addresses itself to the intelligence but even more to the heart. Just like fire warms the heart, the Holy Spirit makes us feel God's presence.

Saint Thomas writes about the unhappiness of someone who ignores the feeling of God's presence with terms that he borrowed from the elder Tobit who lamented about his blindness: "...what joy is left for me anymore? I am a man without eyesight; I cannot see the light of heaven, but I lie in darkness like the dead who no

longer see the light. Although still alive, I am among the dead"
(Tob 5:10). If God is life, then his absence is death, the absence of
his light, or the shadows of atheism, a tomb.

The light of God leads man onto the right path. The Hebrews
crossed the desert by the light of the pillar of fire at night (See Ex
13:21), so they could travel by both day and night. They should
then spiritually be imitated for the prophet Isaiah also invited
them to walk in the light of God: "Nations shall come to your
light, and kings to the brightness of your dawn" (Isa 60:3). Our
mangers, the images of adoration for the wise men at the end of
their journey to the star, remind us of this.

The Holy Spirit, then, directs man's journey. Many times, Saint
Paul had this experience during his missionary voyages, in particular when he arrived in Macedonia (Acts 16:9). The apostles
did also, by obeying God rather than man. They followed their
Master, for Jesus had always acted according to the impetus of
the Holy Spirit: led by the Spirit, he entered the wilderness (Lk
4:1), came to be baptized by John (Lk 3:22), and at the end of his
earthly life, went to Jerusalem. Spirit of fire, Spirit of God!

Fire warms bodies and hearts, perhaps that is its most emo-
tional aspect. A fire that smolders, keeps its heat, a life-giving
heat, localized, enclosed, closed in a small space. It evokes an
image of the feathers of a mother hen who gathers and warms her
baby chicks! Its aspect of security is not excluded either! Thus
God, through his Holy Spirit, gives life to the universe.

At the time of creation, the Holy Spirit covered the waters
and the "tohu-bohu" (earth without form) by giving birth to the
divine Word and giving life to all beings. All new births would see
the presence of the Holy Spirit. In the history of Israel, the coming of the reign of the judges, like that of the prophets and kings,
would see the Holy Spirit of God at work, swooping down on
some, anointing others, all would be established in and consecrated to their own functions by the Holy Spirit. Far from falling
short of this law, the new creation participated in it to a large
degree. The Holy Spirit descended upon Mary: "...the power of

the Most High will overshadow you...the child to be born will be holy; he will be called Son of God" (Lk 1:35). The Word was made flesh and those who wanted to be reborn in God, to become children of God, must believe in his Name, accept the light of the Holy Spirit and its life-giving warmth: the chrismal unction of baptism.

In the Upper Chamber (of the Lord's Supper), we find, at the time of the Pentecost, a place where it seems that the Holy Spirit appears in order to teach and strengthen the apostles as well as give life to the birth of the Church: "Divided tongues, as of fire, appeared among them" (Acts 2:3). This theophany (visible manifestation of God), or pneumatophany (giving the breath of life), gathers all of the characteristics of the divine fire together. The Pentecost is the feast of the Holy Spirit and the divine fire, par excellence!

The apostles still needed to be purified. Not long before, they had discussed who would be greater in the kingdom of heaven, certain proof of an imperfect understanding of the Christian revelation. Fire purifies. God's judgment, before being punishment and destruction, is purification by fire. The divine fire creates: it begets, incubates, and purifies. Saint Thomas tells us that the world will be purified by fire. The apostles experienced it and we will as well.

The feast of the Pentecost invites us also to look at another aspect of fire that was brought to the forefront by the Angelic Doctor: "fire enflames." On the day following the Pentecost, the apostles were unrecognizable! A dry piece of kindling thrown onto the fire catches fire...thus, the apostles, fifty days after Easter, went from the fear of the Jews, to the challenge, to boldness. They met with tribunals, prison, and torture. "We cannot keep from speaking about what we have seen and heard" (Acts 4:20). Such is the transformation caused by the fire of the Holy Spirit in whoever delivers oneself to him.

Saint Thomas sets a trap when he declares that it is a devastating fire. We cannot deny this aspect of fire, but is God devastating? The Angelic Doctor invokes a passage from Deuteronomy: "for a fire is kindled by my anger, and burns to the depths of Sheol" (Deut 32:22). Two interpretations seem possible: one allusion is to the eternal fire of hell that bursts forth less from the wrath of God than his justice. It represents the desperation caused by their eternal separation from God, specific to the outcasts who refuse all mercy. We can, however, consider God himself like a devastating fire who is, at the same time, a purifier, the purification being the elimination of all that is foreign. God's holiness is incompatible with sin. In order to reach the vision of God, purification must then be perfect. The action of the Holy Spirit destroys sin in us by consuming it.

The divine fire, remarked Saint Thomas, changes all things in him: wood becomes fire, the heated and incandescent iron becomes fire, and so on. Under the action of the Holy Spirit, man becomes a spark of God, a particle of the divine fire, its rebirth or filiation in the Son with respect to the Father is the work of the Holy Spirit. God, love, and charity transforms the Christian in as much as he is united with and is open to his action. Come Spirit of fire, Spirit of God!

Paradoxically, the fire of the Holy Spirit that reveals itself to be devastating when faced with sin also appears to be gentle. The God of Moses, arisen up in a storm, revealed himself to Elijah in a gentle breeze (See 1 Kings 19). A destroyer of sin, it builds the Christian up with pedagogy and attention. Jesus said: "And I, when I am lifted up from the earth, will draw all people to myself" (Jn 12:32), and through his Holy Spirit, he realized his promise. Just like fire draws towards the highest flames, sparks and burning embers, thus the Holy Spirit leads souls to the Father. By commenting on Isaiah 30:27: "the name of the Lord comes from far away...his tongue is like a devouring fire," Saint Thomas reminds us that charity is a fire that illuminates intelligence, warms the heart, converts everything in itself, and draws all to God. He cites the canticle: "Upon my bed at night I sought him whom my soul loves..." (Song 3:1). It is not on earth that we must seek

God, but "from above": "Seek the one who is from above." In a
marital context, the soul is drawn to and seeks the one it loves up
above. With sweetness and strength, the Holy Spirit exerts his
attraction on the Christian soul and draws it to the heart of God
in the Holy Trinity.

"King of Heaven, Consoler,
Spirit of Truth,
You who are present everywhere and who fills
everything up with a
Treasure of goods and Giver of Life,
Come and dwell in us."

REFLECTION QUESTIONS

In what ways do I feel the Holy Spirit working within me in my
daily life? Do I feel the Spirit's guiding light as I seek to know and
understand God's will in my life? Do I feel the Spirit's purifying
power during the sacrament of reconciliation and in the penance
that follows? Do I feel the Spirit's transforming power as I seek to
be a better, more courageous, and outspoken Christian? Do I feel
the Spirit's deep love within my heart, and the peace that accom-
panies that love?

DAY EIGHT

The Blessed Virgin Mary

FOCUS POINT

"Hail Mary, full of grace...." Specifically, Mary was graced in three major ways, according to Saint Thomas. First, she was conceived without sin, so that her womb would be free of iniquity and worthy of the Lord. Second, Mary was graced in the Incarnation, as she gave birth to the Son of God, raising him with her great love. Finally, Mary was graced in the Assumption, in which she was assumed body and soul into heaven, to share in the love of God for all eternity and aid those on earth in acquiring God's grace by her intercession.

"Then the cloud covered the tent of meeting, and the glory of the Lord filled the tabernacle" (Ex 40:34).

"The Holy Spirit will come upon you, and the power of the Most High will overshadow you" (Lk 1:35).

It is not by commenting on the "You are most beautiful, Virgin Mary" of the feast of the Immaculate Conception, but with respect to Matthew 1:24–25: "...Joseph took her as his wife, but had no marital relations with her until she had borne a son" that the Angelic Doctor speaks of Mary and her virginity. Certain people have concluded from this verse that Joseph later had a marital relationship with Mary after Jesus was born. No. Saint Thomas brings us close to Mary. According to John Chrysostom, in the Marian mystery, after Jesus' birth, Joseph knew Mary, not in a carnal way, but spiritually, as the most beautiful and worthy woman, for only she had carried the One in her womb whom the whole world couldn't contain. Then Thomas continued: *"This exceptional maternity shone on the face of Mary like the prior visit that God made to Moses had made his face radiant.... Thus, Mary, dwelling in the enlightenment of the power of the Most High, could not have known Joseph before she gave birth. But after her delivery, she knew Joseph, not through carnal contact, but by the beauty of his face"* (S.T. IIIa, Q28:3).

A passage from the third book of his *Sentences* explains his thoughts: Mary never knew sin and never had the occasion to know of it: *"the joy of sanctification not only banished all illicit movements in her, but it also had a repercussion of sorts with others in that even though she was corporally very beautiful, she was not desired by anyone"* (III *Sentences* 3, Q1:2, Q1:4). This is a grace that is similar to that which appeared in the life of Joan of Arc, who lived for a time amongst soldiers with neither desire, nor occasion of desire.

The Bible knew many saints who were sanctified while in their mother's wombs: *"John the Baptist is greater than Jeremiah, but Mary surpassed them both: John the Baptist and Jeremiah had been chosen as particular prefigurations to the sanctification of Christ...and they did not know grave sins, the grace of God protected them.... But the Virgin had been kept from all sins, even venial ones, through a greater grace, for she had been chosen to be the Mother of God"* (S.T. IIIa, Q27:6, 1).

"Hail Mary, full of grace…." If Thomas had given the absolute fullness of grace to Mary, what would there be left for Christ in his humanity? Mary, then, only received a plenitude of grace that was relative to, and corresponded to, her mission. Just as Saint Stephen is said to be *"filled with grace"* in order to respond to his vocation as a deacon or servant, a witness to God and protomartyr, *"in the same way, Mary was filled with grace in this sense that she had sufficient grace for the vocation to which she had been called by God: to be the Mother of God"* (S.T. IIIa, Q7:11, 1).

Grace, like God's glance, was placed on Mary from that first instant and follows her throughout her existence on earth and in heaven. Mary's first grace was of predestination. Her divine maternity demanded great purity and exempted Mary from all sins, either those that were committed or "received." *"The second perfection of the grace was within the Blessed Virgin Mary from the time of the presence of the Son of God incarnated in her womb."* With a scientific dryness, Thomas announced the fact and then continued: *"The third perfection of the grace in Mary is the one of her final end which she has in glory"* (S.T. IIIa, Q27:5, 2). In a few lines, the Angelic Doctor brought the plenitude of Mary's grace to the Immaculate Conception, the Incarnation, and the Assumption! This triple gift of graces attaches itself to the triple freedoms of Mary and to three successive commitments to good. From the time of her conception, she was kept from all sin, after the Annunciation, the presence of Jesus in her purified her tendencies and confirmed her in goodness, her assumption finally freed her from the miserable conditions of our world and gave her the rejoicing of all goodness in God.

Mary is not an angel but the Queen of the angels. Created above them, she had been ranked higher than them; their respectful inclination before her does not arise from either iconography, or Mariolatry, or from an exaggerated pious fervor, but from authentic theology. *"Since she was a woman and because of that state of life, she was inferior to angels. Even Christ, in his human-*

ity, is said to be inferior to the angels (See Heb 2:9).... Mary also needed to be instructed by the angels about God's plans.... The Mother of God was superior to the angels by the dignity by which she had been divinely chosen" (S.T. IIIa, Q30:2, 1).

When Thomas read the gospel story about Martha and Mary (See Lk 10:41) on the occasion of a wedding, it brought him to ask himself about Mary's active and contemplative life. Her active home life would predispose her to the contemplation of the marvels of God in his Son and in her according to the principle of "he who first conducts himself well reaches the contemplative life in good condition." The effort required to practice virtue could cause problems for contemplation but we assume that Mary accomplished her daily duties easily and with love and that never caused any shyness for her meditation of the events in her heart (See III *Sentences* D. 35, Q1:art III, 2).

Was Mary sanctified after her birth or in her mother's womb? Must we situate this sanctification *in utero*, before or after the giving of life to her body? Curiously, Thomas remarked that Mary is the Tabernacle of the New Covenant, noted in the Old Testament by the meeting tent, and that she had been consecrated only after her completion. He concluded that Mary had been consecrated at the moment of the giving of life to her body. Before that time, not having yet become human, she could not have received this grace; and after, she would have been in sin for a certain amount of time which would be contrary to our belief. Her sanctification, then, occurred when she was given life.

The Church declared that Mary was "preserved" from original sin rather than "redeemed" from it; the principle that "Christ is the savior for all man" remains valid for Mary even if, in this case, it takes on an aspect of preservation.

Mary's faith remains a model for all Christians: *"Doubt brings with it a weakness of faith. It can't exist without sin. Even at the time of the Passion, doubt never invaded Mary; her faith remained extremely strong, even if the apostles had doubts."* On the other hand, Thomas granted her a *"doubt of amazement or admiration when she considered that he had been treated so very badly when she had so miraculously given birth to him"* (III *Sentences* DIII, Q1:art II; Q2:1). Perhaps this is the meaning of our *pietas*? This faith, very strong, that Thomas found in Mary at the Passion should be projected on the entirety of the lives of Mary and Jesus. The growth of faith, like that of her grace, was a plenitude by corresponding at each moment to the concrete situation.

Mary's purity was total, right from the time of her birth and it never changed. At the absolute of the absence of sin, comes that of purity. To the contrary, *"In Mary, there exists a growth of charity since that is an approach and participation in the (Divine) Love that is God; the Virgin Mary did not have the greatest charity, the one beyond which we can't imagine, but she always progressed in her charity. It is the same with her grace"* (III *Sentences* D. 17, Q2:3).

Mary also possessed the gift of Wisdom, not in its totality but with respect to her vocation. She experienced, to the maximum, the mysteries to which she was intimately connected; however, she was not ever given to teach. The reason brought to the forefront by Saint Thomas, repeating Saint Paul, is far from satisfactory: "I permit no woman to teach" (1 Tim 2:12). It just underlines the problems. In the same way, in her lifetime, Mary did not seem to have performed miracles, yet after her Assumption, she seems to have made up for lost time! It was up to Christ and his disciples to teach and confirm their doctrines through miracles for they alone had been given the responsibility to teach the Good News (See S.T. IIIa, Q27:5, 3). It is the mystery of men and women whose equality implies neither reciprocity not equivalence.

Mary is called the Mother of God, yet never "Mother of the divinity," nor "Mother of the deity." The words God, divinity, and deity signify the same things: God himself, but under two different aspects. "God" signifies the divine nature concretely possessed and personalized. In this sense, Mary is the Mother of God. "Divinity" or "deity" signifies God in his abstract nature, in this sense, Mary is not the Mother of the divine nature, did not engender the deity, and the name is not acceptable. "Mother of God" is in Greek *Theotokos*. We also use the expression "Mother of Christ" whereas the Eastern Rites never use its Greek translation *Christotokos* for historical reasons. *"Nestorius, the heretic, used it...to avoid the use of 'Theotokos' which he refused, by making Jesus a human Messiah and not the Son of God"* (III *Sentences* D4, Q2:2, 5). The expression "Mary, Mother of God" signifies that Mary is the mother of this divine concrete nature that the Son of God assumed at the Incarnation.

The Virgin Mary is called "a branch of Jesse," the expression coming from Isaiah (11:1): "A shoot shall come out from the stump of Jesse and a branch (and a flower) shall grow out of his roots." The context is messianic, Mary is the branch, Jesus is the flower. Saint Thomas didn't stop at the proximity of the Latin words "virgo-virga" (virgin-branch) but brought his attention to the Old Testament. The branch that carried Moses and Aaron at the time of the Exodus, and with which they fulfilled the marvels, was the instrument chosen by God to save his people. Mary is the instrument chosen by God with which Jesus, the new Moses (or great priest), will save mankind. In this branch, Thomas first discerns a characteristic *"of consolation in tribulations"* for, the Hebrew people, being blocked between the Red Sea and the Egyptian army, Moses received the command: "lift up your staff and stretch out your hand over the sea and divide it" (Ex 14:16). Our Lady, consoler of the afflicted!

The branch also brings an aspect of fortification; Thomas discovered it in the Book of Numbers in which the branch represented the family of Aaron, which, while enclosed in the meeting tent, flowered, budded, and bore fruit while that of other families dried up (17:16–26). The greatness of Mary is due to the fruit of her womb. In the third place, Thomas saw in the staff of Moses a *"withering or thirst"* and referred it to the scene in Meribah (See Num 20). Moses struck the rock and water flowed from it. Mary gave to the Church the One whose Body would be its food and whose Blood, a beverage. The Bread of Life descended from heaven and the Source of the Living Waters. Then comes the aspect of *"punishment,"* referred to in the fourth oracle of Balaam: "...a star shall come out of Jacob, and a scepter shall rise out of Israel; it shall crush the borderlands of Moab, and the territory of all the Shethites" (Num 24:17).

Finally, a last aspect of this branch of Jesse compares her to "a keeper of a vigil" and the Angelic Doctor refers it back to the story of Jeremiah's vocation: "What do you see, Jeremiah? I see a branch of the almond tree." Mary is the dawn of salvation, the first light of the "Light of the World."

At the beginning of chapter sixteen of the Book of Isaiah, we read, "Send lambs to the ruler of the land...by way of the desert...," a messianic text that makes the Messiah come from the desert. Thomas did not hesitate to make his geographical connections: *"The Lord is the Father, the lamb is Christ, the jewel of the desert is the nation of Ruth whose people are the jewels since they adore the gods made of jewels."* Then he draws our attention to the lamb who is Christ, *"because of the purity of his life, his gentleness, the humility which he showed in his Passion, and finally because of his redemptive character."* According to this, if the Lamb comes, the expression could only refer to Mary. *"Mary is called the jewel of the desert because of the strength of her faith and grace, in the first place...then, because of her chastity."* Finally, and above all, because of Jesus. Thomas had read in Job 39: "he is spread in a river of oil," Christ is the anointed Lord. If Mary is called the jewel of the desert, it is because of her consecration in grace, her virginity, and her maternity towards the Son of God, the Messiah.

> *"Mother most pure, Mother conceived without sin,*
> *Pray for us.*
> *Mystical Rose—Branch of Jesse,*
> *Pray for us.*
> *Mother full of grace—Queen lifted to heaven*
> *Pray for us"* (Litany of the Holy Virgin).

REFLECTION QUESTIONS

In what ways do I honor Mary in my prayer life and in my daily life? Do I say the rosary? Do I attend Masses in her honor? Do I pray, employing Mary as an intercessor so that she might present my petitions to her Son? Do I practice *lectio divina*, using those parts of Scripture that relate directly to Mary? Do I seek to learn more about Mary, by studying the appropriate parts of the Catechism and related Church doctrine?

DAY NINE

The Birth of Jesus

FOCUS POINT

In the Incarnation, the Word descended into our world and became flesh. This was an act of great humility on the part of the Divine, that he would lower himself to the level of man, that the eternal would become temporal. This humility in the Incarnation would only be the beginning of the abasement that Jesus Christ would live out in his earthly existence as a servant to all mankind. Jesus Christ is the Son of God and the son of Mary, and in this one Person of Christ there is a union of the two natures, divine and human.

"When the fullness of time had come, God sent his Son, born of a woman" (Gal 4:4).

"The Apostles' Creed affirms that Christ was conceived by the power of the Holy Spirit. In the Nicene Creed, we find 'he was begotten by the power of the Holy Spirit...and became man'

so that we see that he did not take on an imaginary body (according to the Manicheans), but one of real flesh.... We add, 'he descended from heaven' in order to refute the errors made by those who affirm that Christ was purely a man, by saying that he drew his beginnings from Mary so that, through the merit of a good life having been begun on earth, he would ascend to heaven rather than, being of a celestial origin, taking on flesh, he would have descended onto the earth" (C., I, 220).

Putting aside the controversial aspect of Thomas's text, we will examine the depths of the mysteries of the Incarnation that circumstances brought Thomas to clarify. We believe that Jesus is truly both God and man—how can that be, how could that have been realized?

It is appropriate that the Redeemer of the human race was a man, God saving humanity with its own collaboration. It could have been otherwise but God chose this path. Jesus descended from Adam through his mother, the genealogies that were reported by Saint Matthew and again by Saint Luke showed this: the descendants of Adam would be saved.

In order to destroy sin, the Redeemer was born without sin and never knew it. The original sin that is transmitted through natural generation was not applicable to the Redeemer. He was born of a woman who was supernaturally impregnated by God. The phrase "begotten by God" refers back to the common divine activity of the Father, Son, and Holy Spirit in their omnipotence. Saint Luke speaks specifically of the Holy Spirit but let us not conclude from it that he would be the father of Jesus. The mention of it comes from the appropriation or attribution to one of the divine Persons, for a particular reason, of a common action of the three Persons. Considered as the effector of great divine actions: creation, re-creation, sanctification, the impregnation of Mary is attributed to him (the Holy Spirit). In the Holy Trinity, the Holy Spirit originates from the Father and the Son, he could not be the Father of the latter, even at the time of the Incarnation.

Jesus has no other father than the Father; for all eternity, he begets him: "*Hodie genuui te*—today, I beget you." In the Incarnation, this generation takes on a new form: eternal, it goes beyond time. Divine and spiritual, it becomes something other than human and carnal. Nevertheless, it remains that the two terms of the relationship are the same, the Persons of the Father and Son, even if the generation unfolds as eternal and temporal.

The natural phenomenon of human conception is better known in our era than it was in Saint Thomas's time, but there were already questions being asked then about the time of his coming to life. To this can be added, for the Incarnation, the time of his deification. Did God deify a child that had already been conceived? No, Mary never had a purely human child that wasn't, from the very first moment, the Son of God. Let us retain, along with Saint Thomas and Christian tradition, the simultaneousness of his coming to life and his deification, or of the "formation" of the body by the soul and the assumption of human nature, thus formed by the Person of the Son. Thomas insists upon this simultaneousness without which Mary would be neither a virgin nor the Mother of God. Christian faith says that: "*God made himself become a man*" or "*the Word was made flesh*" and not that "*a man made himself become God.*" "*If the deification had taken place after conception, then for a certain period of time, Mary would have been the mother of a man whose person would not have been that of the Word of God*" (S.T. IIIa, Q33:3).

The phrase "*descendit des coelis*—he descended from heaven" shows the Incarnation to have been like a "descent" of the Word of God into our carnal world and not like the "ascent" of a human being in divinity. This descent constitutes the "kenosis" or voluntary and humble abasement of the Word, a prelude to the humility of his earthly life, of his condition as a servant and that as a condemned person. "*God made himself become a man, it was not man who became God*" (S.T. IIIa, Q16:6, 7).

A certain inconsistency arises: God could not make himself come to life. The mystery of eternity penetrates time. By taking on a human nature, God could come to life, be born, grow, and so on. *"God could not become a man for all eternity but only in time (for a certain time period), then he became a man."* By doing this, God gives us the possibility of participating in his divinity.

Through a hypostatic union (that is, in the Person), the Word of God unites himself with Mary's human nature. In the Person of Christ, the two natures, divine and human, are united. *"In this conception, there are many things that come from the (human) nature and many others that are beyond it, supernatural"* (S.T. IIIa, Q33:4 RD). *"From Mary's side, everything is natural, but from the side of the active power, everything is miraculous. This conception of Christ must also be considered, first, as miraculous and supernatural and, only second, as natural"* (Ibid).

In the Gospel, we often encounter the expression: "the Son of man"—Jesus even used it to refer to himself. Saint Thomas notes that Christ was not the "son of a man," not having had a human father (not considering his adoptive or legal father), but he is "the son of man," or of the human nature that he received from Mary.

Right from the first moment that Mary carried the Son of God within her: *"At the first moment of his conception, the Word had given life to the body of Christ and assumed him…and consequently, at the first moment of his conception, Christ had the plenitude of graces that sanctified his body and his soul"* (S.T. IIIa, Q34:1 RD). Who will speak of the holiness of Jesus, the source of our own?

At Christmastime, the Son of God was born in Bethlehem. Habit masks the strangeness of the proposition. A birth is attributed to a person. Mary and Joseph could have announced the birth of Jesus. This birth introduced the Son of God into a life that was of this world, human, like our own, yet the Eternal Word of God remained eternal and unchanged, for he was God!

Did Mary confer existence on him? The mystery is great, it is the very mystery of Christ. Mary did not give existence, in the absolute sense of the word, to the Word of God since *"he exists"* for all eternity, but she gave him *"human existence."* Not *"to be"* but *"to be a man,"* for through her, the One who exists for all eternity became a man. Jesus only ever had one existence, an eternal and divine one, which, at a certain moment, duplicated itself into a temporal human form. Jesus doesn't have two *"esse—existences,"* but only one, in two forms. That gives Jesus' affirmation, "before Abraham, I existed," an infinite and divine significance. The Jews were not wrong there. The newborn child existed for all eternity; his "human existence" began, installed in a period of time, would border on his "Godly existence" and that would never be modified. There should never be a mix-up or confusion between his human existence and Godly existence, with the unity of the unique Person of the Son of God.

All children are adorable in the eyes of their mothers, but the expression here has taken on a broader meaning. Jesus is adorable in the strictest sense of the word. Adoration is given to a divine Person: the Father, Son, or Holy Spirit—God. In Jesus, it addresses itself to the Son of God who is, so to speak, adorable.

Jesus is the son of Mary and of the Father; he is the son of both, but in very different ways: in eternity—the Son of the Father; in time—the son of Mary. Divinely, he is the Son of the Father and humanly, the son of Mary. Each man is the son of his father and his mother, a single filiation puts him into a relationship with each of his parents, just like a single conception, one unique birth, made him the son of both of them. Saint Thomas said that Jesus is not the son of Mary and the Son of the Father through a unique filiation, for, in the first place, the eternal generation of the Word by the Father was totally different from that of Mary which was temporal. Temporal and eternal generations and eternal and temporal births differ from each other and even Jesus' filiations do with respect to his Father and his mother. However, Thomas turned to the Persons: that of the Son, the Father, and Mary and seems to see, in Jesus, only one filiation by making him the Son of Mary and the Father.

The Son of God became the son of Mary: what "impact" does this fact have on the Person of the Son? Would the Incarnation modify his eternal reality? Saint Thomas tells us: *"The filiation that puts Christ into a relationship with his mother could not be a real relationship but only one of reason"* (S.T. IIIa, Q35:5 RD). Let us not get caught up in the words. The Jesus-Mary filiation, created, in Mary, a real relationship of maternity: Jesus is fully her Son and she his Mother; but, conversely, the same relationship could not, in any way, change the divinity of the Son of God. Creation did not change God, neither did the Incarnation. Incarnate, the Word remained in his divinity the All-Other, the Unchangeable and unchanged, the mystery of the Infinite One to whom anything added or taken away changes nothing. In Bethlehem, at Jesus' birth, the Word of God was in him, he was him, without the least modification in his divinity, "next to the Father."

The shepherds and the wise men were the first adorers of Christ, they all came to Bethlehem, saw the child with his mother, and adored him. Saint Thomas explained that Christ, by coming to save the world through faith in him, *"had to manifest the birth of Christ in such a way that the revelation of his divinity did no harm in any way to that of his humanity...on one hand, Christ carried the misery of the human condition within himself and yet, the power of his divinity had been revealed by the creatures of God"* (S.T. IIIa Q36:4 RD). Thus, at the beginning of his life, Christ appeared like a man and had only been perceived to be God through the witness of the angels and the stars. Later, when he was well integrated with mankind, he revealed himself to be the Son of God through his teachings and miracles. The Apostles had met a man, followed him, listened to him, and discerned, after his death and resurrection, that he was the Son of God. Saint John's Gospel makes clear there is also an "ascending" Christology rising from humanity to the divinity of Jesus. But the fourth gospel proposes a descending Christology of the Word of God to Jesus of Nazareth "highlighting the condescendence of divine mercy."

"The Word was made flesh
and he dwelled amongst us." (Jn 1:14)

REFLECTION QUESTIONS

Do I regularly contemplate the Mysteries, specifically the Incarnation, in my prayer life? Do I tend to think of Jesus more according to his divine nature than his human nature, or vice versa? Why might I tend to think of him one way rather than another? How does this affect the way I approach Jesus in prayer? What spiritual writers might I pursue to help me in gaining a better understanding of Jesus' dual natures?

The Growth of Jesus

FOCUS POINT

All the love we have for others, all the love that we direct toward them, comes from the Source of all love: Jesus Christ. We have been divinized by his Incarnation, by his great love for all of us. We recognize him in our neighbor and seek to serve our neighbor, to love our neighbor, because of the love of Jesus Christ inside of us, that moves us to love the good in those around us. As the Church, we are the Body and Jesus is the head, directing all his graces from the head throughout the body.

"The righteous flourish like the palm tree, and grow like a cedar in Lebanon" (Ps 92:12–13).

Did Jesus know me when he was on earth? Does he know me naturally? Such is the kind of question that I ask myself, not without some concern; could this man who lived some two thousand years ago have known me and if he didn't know me what use do I have for Christian faith? Saint Thomas affirms that *"the soul of Christ knows, in the Word, all of the realities of each moment as they exist and even men's thoughts, of which he is the judge"* (S.T. IIIa, Q10:2 RD).

How could this child perceive of the mystery of his destiny and of his own being? Born in Bethlehem, how could he, some twelve years later, say to his parents: "Did you not know that I must be in my Father's house?" (Lk 2:49). Jesus is the Word of God and enjoys perfect, divine knowledge of all things, but this does not interfere with his own human knowledge. As well as this divine knowledge, Christ has another, imperfect and partial, because it is human, that he either acquired by experience or received from God. It belongs to his human nature and without it *"his human soul would not have been perfect...if he had had normal human intelligence that would not have functioned, he would have been frustrated...to know is a part of the concept of an animal with the power of reason"* (S.T. IIIa, Q9:1 RD).

Human knowledge that is influenced by divine knowledge is conflicting to their non-confusion, just like all interference of the divine nature in the human is. The Council of Chalcedon and the third Council of Constantinople teaches that Jesus is perfectly a man and completely God without the confusion of either their natures or kinds of knowledge.

A viewpoint that is a little "maximalist" of the Incarnation, insists Saint Thomas, grants Christ the highest human knowledge, right from the time of his earthly life (and even from his conception), not just after his resurrection: Christ must have had a humanity that was the most perfect. The beatific viewpoint, that of God and all things in him, the gift of God to the chosen people is the highest knowledge, supernatural, for no one could acquire it through his own means, even if man, in his very nature, is made for God (in his image) and possesses a certain aptitude to receive this knowledge. For reasons of expediency, Saint Thomas adds another: no one can give what he doesn't have: *"Man is empowered with the gift for the knowledge of those who are blessed, that is, to see God, and is called to this vision as his life's goal. He is a being with the power to reason, gifted with this blessed vision through the humanity of Christ...that is why it is good that this knowledge, which consists of seeing God, agrees perfectly with Christ in his humanity"* (S.T. IIIa, Q9:2 RD).

Faced with the impossibility of representing ourselves as knowing everyone from all periods of time and places, we could only attempt an approach. Mary, the mother of Jesus, lifted to heaven, now enjoys this vision. She knows all people. Each person, in the universality of time and place, can invoke her and receive an answer from her. To those who are especially privileged, she appears, as much in Europe as in other places, speaking their own languages. In the same way, the saints in heaven know all who invoke them, no matter when and from what place. Would Jesus have had this knowledge before his Passion, all throughout his earthly life? The expression that we attribute to him, "I shed my blood for you," should then be taken in its strictest sense. Saint Thomas was not always understood by everyone on this. It was brought to our attention that it is the risen Christ who leads man to the blessed vision; to give it to him after his resurrection raised no further objections. Moreover, Jesus is perfectly a man, and the vision of God *"antemortem"* seems to be beyond his limitations, even if it pleases God to enlarge on them. On the other hand, Thomas is categorical on this point and affirms, on numerous occasions, the beatific vision that Christ had on earth. Only the fact that his body had not been glorified differentiated him from the chosen ones.

Like all men, Jesus acquired knowledge through experience over time; he was gifted with intelligence and will; we must not lessen or overestimate this fact: *"The Son of God took on a completely human nature with a soul that could feel and reason; he must have, then, possessed knowledge created for the perfection of his soul...and that of his intelligence"* (S.T. IIIa, Q9:1 RD).

Saint Luke writes that Jesus grew in age, wisdom, and grace before God and man (2:52). Based upon this affirmation, Thomas concluded: *"Christ grew in wisdom and in grace, as well as in years, for as he grew in age, he did greater deeds which manifested a higher level of knowledge and grace"* (S.T. IIIa, Q12:2 RD). Then he came back to the question of the growth of Christ's knowledge and whether it was acquired or gained through experience: *"This knowledge was always perfect, relative to Christ's age; it was neither absolutely nor essentially perfect, and that is why it could progress"* (Ibid). We grasp the care that the Angelic Doctor took to give Christ perfect knowledge, but a perfection of knowledge that was relevant to his age. The Son of God and the son of a carpenter, Jesus is both God and man.

The first experiences that Jesus had were with his parents. Just like all other children, he must have called Mary and Joseph "mama" and "daddy." In Joseph's house, the ambiguity of the term could have only coexisted with the righteousness of the just (man) with some difficulty. We could think that he set things straight in the mind of the young child early on. The term "mama" addressed to Mary did not have to hurdle the same obstacle and corresponded to the truth, however the exceptional family situation could not have been compared by the child to the current situation for a long time. The family context helped the child to situate himself in truth. Here, another form of knowledge is introduced, one that is more or less developed in all people, infused knowledge that is directly given by God.

While still very young, Jesus was introduced to "the Law, the Prophets, and other writings." At the age of thirty, he taught as a master in the synagogue in Nazareth, but much earlier on, at the age of twelve, he was noted for his great knowledge of Judaism. Mary and Joseph found him in the Temple "sitting among the teachers, listening to them and asking them questions. And all who heard him were amazed at his understanding and his answers" (Lk 2:46–47). Without a doubt, the religious education, in this particular case, was multiplied with an uncommon, exceptional infused knowledge. Rapidly, the student would have gone beyond the teacher, the child, his parents. The end of Luke's Gospel, the episode with the pilgrims of Emmaus, shows us Jesus' progression in his knowledge of the Scriptures and, particularly, in those which concerned him.

As a child, Jesus must have discovered his own personality, his personal being, his sense of self; he could have brought closer the prophecies of the Emmanuel of the words of his mother. The expression "Abba-Father," misused with respect to Joseph, found a completely different resonance in Jesus' prayer, a bounty of truth.

Saint Thomas granted Jesus the greatest infused knowledge possible: *"We read in Isaiah (11:2) 'The spirit of the Lord shall rest on him, the spirit of wisdom and understanding, the spirit of counsel and might, the spirit of knowledge and the fear of the Lord.' In these lines, we must discern all objects of knowledge: from Wisdom, comes knowledge of divine things; to intelligence, that of nonmaterial reality; to knowledge, that of all conclusions; to counsel, those of practical things. It seems, then, that Christ, through the infused knowledge that the Holy Spirit communicated to him, knew everything"* (S.T. IIIa, Q111:1).

The prayer of Jesus as a child must have been the special place of his discovery of his soul and personality. It is difficult to imagine this prayer. "Blessed are the pure in heart, for they will see God" (Mt 5:8). The very pure heart of Jesus "saw God" very early on, first in a beatific vision and through the gift of the highest Wisdom. It was there that he must have become humanly conscious of his identity as the Son of God. Saint Thomas tells us that this recognition: *"was not discursive* (arrived at through reasoning or argument) *for it was not acquired through personal experience, but divinely infused"* (S.T. IIIa Q11:3 RD). We can picture Jesus receiving this discovery through prayer rather than through deductive reasoning. In the same way, prayer reveals our divine filiation to us and makes us recognize God as our Father.

Saint John wrote: "...we have seen his glory...full of grace and truth" (1:14) with respect to Jesus, the Word of God who came to our world. If grace is a benevolent glance, a smile from God, his Son, in whom the Father was pleased, could only be full of grace. It is through grace that the Word was made flesh, that he assumed our human nature by being born of Mary; the fruit of the womb of this Mother, Virgin, could only be blessed. Son of God, he had all of God's kindnesses, and all of his grace reflected upon his humanity: *"We must distinguish a double grace in Christ. First, that of union, the human nature of Jesus being connected to his divine nature in the Person of the Son. This grace is as infinite as the Person of the Word. The second is the usual grace..."* (S.T. IIIa, Q7:11 RD).

We must never forget the realism of the Incarnation that was so well noted by Saint John: "We declare to you what was from the beginning, what we have heard, what we have seen with our eyes, what we have looked at and touched with our hands, concerning the word of life" (1 Jn 1:1). The flesh of the Word of life could only be filled with grace, with an infinite grace, since it addresses itself to God in the Person of the Son: the Incarnation of divine love that the Father has for his Son.

Saint Thomas also spoke about usual grace in Jesus, he sees it as something infinite since it is the smile of the Father, his glance or the love of the Father for this man who is his Son. However, objectively, in Jesus' soul, this grace remains limited to the size of his soul. *"Usual grace could be considered to be something that was created, limited, finite. It dwells in Christ's soul. He is a creature, of limited capacities. Thus, the grace is, in this aspect, limited. But according to its nature as a grace, it is infinite, unlimited"* (S.T. IIIa, Q7:11 RD). This same grace is reflected in us.

Jesus is the head of the Mystical Body that is the Church and, in this body, grace flows from the head towards its parts. All of the grace that I receive comes to me from Christ. It flows from him to me, just like the sap flows to the shoots, to give me life, deify me, and make me conform to him. Saint John sums up this

Paulist thought by writing: "From his fullness we have all received, grace upon grace" (Jn 1:16). Saint Thomas explains that the grace that Christ received in plenitude is spread out over us all: *"Christ's soul received the maximum amount of grace. That is why, from this maximum of grace that he received, it is agreed that this grace reflects back on all the others..."* (S.T. IIIa, Q8:5 RD). It is, then, from the same love by which the Father loves his Son, for all eternity, that he loves each and every man, united to his Son.

Jesus, conscious of your existence, your mission and with a clarity that is always growing, you gave yourself for all mankind. You were completely conscious of the universality of this mission. What is it to love all mankind? Does love have to be recognized? There exists a love of things that is only glimpsed. Existential charity from certain souls leads us to believe that "love is without boundaries." If a Saint Vincent de Paul or a Mother Teresa of Calcutta had loved their neighbor with such great love, it came directly from the heart of Jesus. Therefore it follows, this divine heart contains the love of all of those who, in the world and across the centuries, truly loved.

> "The door is the way by which all enter
> into the house.
> Only Christ is the one through whom we have access
> to the grace in which we dwell" (S.T. IIIa, Q8:7, 3).

REFLECTION QUESTIONS

How do I react to those people in my life who are difficult, who do not share my views and opinions on matters that are important to me? Do I react to these people with disdain? Do I avoid them? Do I see only the worst side of them so that I might feel justified in the opinions that I hold? Or do I try to see the Christ that shines inside of them? And do I try to see them with the eyes of Christ, the One who created this person, the One who loves this person so much?

DAY ELEVEN

The Firstborn From the Dead

FOCUS POINT

Through his Incarnation, Jesus sanctified the flesh, which was once strictly in the chains of sin. And when he died, Jesus defeated death by his resurrection. No longer did the sin of Adam prevent the flesh from knowing God in the eternity of heaven. When Jesus conquered death and sanctified the flesh, humanity was reborn, reunited to the divine, and the order of universe—previously flawed by man's sin of pride—was reestablished and set right by the God-Man, Jesus Christ.

"He is the beginning, the firstborn from the dead, so that he might come to have first place in everything. For in him all the fullness of God was pleased to dwell" (Col 1:18–19).

"That he would have wanted to arise on the third day is a mystery in order to show that he was raised from the dead through the virtue of the whole Trinity. From that, we can say that the

*Father raised him from the dead as much as he did himself; it is
also true that it is the same virtue for all three, the Father, Son,
and the Holy Spirit..." (Compendium Theo., 236, 5).*

*"No one takes it (my life) from me, but I lay it down of my
own accord. I have the power to lay it down, and I have the
power to take it up again" (Jn 10:18).*

*"Jesus of Nazareth...this man...who you crucified and killed
by the hands of those outside the law. But God raised him up,
having freed him from death..." (Acts 2:22–24).*

T hese two last passages seem to be contradictory. Will they
make me lose faith in the resurrection of Jesus Christ? Should
I attribute this resurrection, the foundation of my Christian faith,
to Jesus himself as Saint John did? Or do I attribute it to the
Father, following the Acts of the Apostles of Saint Luke? Jesus
was raised from the dead on the third day and he appeared to
especially chosen witnesses; that is certain.

Lord, why were you raised on the third day? The answer can
be found in the Credo: "On the third day he rose again." But it
doesn't satisfy me at all: it compounds the problem! Lord, a certain amount of time was necessary between your death and resurrection, a time that was neither too long nor too short. *"(If it
was) too short, it could seem that his death wasn't real and, consequently, his resurrection wasn't either"* (S.T. IIIa, Q53:2 RD).

Let us put aside, for now, the medical-philosophical questions about the different types of deaths. A man who has been
crucified, stabbed in the heart with a sword, pronounced dead,
and consequently buried in a tomb is a dead man, or rather a
cadaver. These three days prove the authenticity of your death
and resurrection, Lord.

This delay was short enough: three days in our way of count-
ing total only about forty hours (midday Good Friday to Easter
Sunday morning). The faith of the apostles quickly changed: the

"trust" they had in you, which turned to "despair" on Good Friday, was changed to "living faith" on the Sunday morning: "Christ has arisen, he has truly arisen!" If mankind only arises at the end of time, Jesus, you only waited three days! If you had waited until the end of time, how would we have been saved? How could we nourish ourselves of your body, drink of your blood, and bathe in your death and resurrection in order to live the eternal life? Everything came to be realized by his resurrection on the third day.

Lord, why did you arise from the dead in the nighttime, with no witnesses, most probably just at dawn? The gospels don't explain it. Lord, may my curiosity be resolved, but my faith knows that you are the Light of the world and recognizes your victory over the shadows of the physical and cosmological night and, above all, over the nights of sin and death. "The dawn from on high will break upon us, to give light to those of us who sit in the darkness and in the shadow of death" (Lk 1:78–79). Lord, you would have already introduced me into the light of your glory even if it is only through the veil of faith. Dead in the evening, arisen in the morning: a new day of re-Creation. Like days come out of darkness, the arisen Lord springs forth from the tomb. You are the light that is born of the Light, today you illuminate the tomb in which man had buried you.

"[T]his man...you crucified.... God raised him up, having freed him from death" (Acts 2:23, 24). Saint Luke is adamant. By remembering Peter's second discourse to the people, he reuses the same formulation: "...you killed the Author of life, whom God raised from the dead. To this we are witnesses" (Acts 3:15). How could it have been otherwise?

On the cross, Jesus' body was spent, his suffering reached the end of his ability to resist any longer, and finally Jesus "bowed his head and gave up his spirit" (Jn 19:30), his last breath, his soul, and his life. The soul is separate from the body; that is how the reality of the Incarnation, the humanity of Jesus, and his death appear to us. He was truly one of us.

The Resurrection, then, must be attributed to God, to the

Father, for Jesus, in his human nature, no longer existed. In his writing of the Acts, Luke remained a faithful disciple to his master, Saint Paul, and reflected his thoughts: in effect, by writing to the Romans, spoke of "the Spirit of him who raised Jesus from the dead" (Rom 8:11), using an expression that denotes the Father. The act is realized through the glory of the Father and that is found to be increased, enriched, and exalted by the whole world.

To a theology that is somewhat tainted with Jansenism and legalism (adhering to the letter of the law rather than the spirit in which it was written) that shows a Father who is angered, sending his Son to the gallows in order to repair or remit sins, we can and must oppose a theology of grace and love in which the Father, bruised in his Father's heart, raises his Son from a death at the hands of the very people to whom he sent his Son in order to preach conversion. It is a theology that conforms more to the teachings of the gospel of the prodigal child. Thus, Christ opens the doors of resurrection to us, for all of us will arise from the dead.

The same contemplation on the cross could lead us onto a different path. The blood that flows on the limbs, the body, or the cross of Jesus is the blood of Christ, of Jesus, man and God. Jesus' divinity in not located within him, it dwells no more in the soul nor in the body, nor more in the flesh than in the blood. Everything in him is deified by his belonging to the Person of the Word of God. Each drop of his blood carries God in it, the Way of the Cross is marked with traces of God. At the death of Jesus, the soul separated itself from his body in spite of the tension, which was very human, that united them. The divinity found itself torn apart, complete and without change in the body, like in the soul. Feeling this deeply, Thérèse of Lisieux did not want to lose a single drop of the blood of Christ and Thomas Aquinas celebrated the Eucharist with great piety. If the body and soul of Christ claimed kinship, drawing itself together with all of their energy and refused the separation, hence the divinity, attached, one to the other, will react against this separation. Ravished by the violence acted upon his humanity, the divinity could not withstand the trial. If that was the case, right from the very moment of his death, the Resurrection should have had to take place. Man cannot "force" God, but the divine plan carried with it a lapse of time and the Son of God accepted that. On the third day, the power of the divinity of Jesus, the paternal plan no longer making an obstacle, reunited the body and soul and he arose from the dead. This very same power will reunite our souls and our bodies at the end of time.

Jesus said: "For this reason the Father loves me, because I lay down my life in order to take it up again. No one takes it (my life) from me, but I lay it down of my own accord. I have the power to lay it down, and I have the power to take it up again. I have received this command from my Father" (Jn 10:17–18). Saint Thomas permits us to say that Christ, in his humanity and divinity, gave his life; but by his divinity alone, he took it back: *In the name of the divinity which is united to him, the body of Christ took back the soul that it had given up and his soul took back the body that it had left. Saint Paul declared (2 Cor 13:4): 'For he was crucified in weakness, but lives by the power of God.' But if we consider the body and soul of the dead Christ according to created nature, they cannot reunite to each other, it is necessary for Christ to be raised from the dead by God* (S.T. IIIa, Q53:4 RD).

By reciting psalms in his own name and making them his own, Jesus said: "You, Lord, be gracious to me and raise me up" (Ps 41:10). The Messiah asked God (his Father) to raise him from the dead; Saint Thomas explains it: *It was like a man and not like a God that Christ asked, through prayer and merit, for his resurrection* (Ibid).

We put our finger on Christ's humanity by feeling the depth of the need of his soul to turn to his Father, a prelude to: "Father, if you are willing, remove this cup from me" (Lk 22:42). This is a very human prayer from Christ which is proven by the blood and sweat that accompanied it. The author of the Epistle to the Hebrews entered into this perspective when he wrote of Christ: "In the days of his flesh, Jesus offered up prayers and supplications with loud cries and tears, to the one who was able to save him from death, and he was heard because of his reverent submission" (Heb 5:7). Christ, in his humanity, suffered and prayed to the Father, who answered him, not by the suppression of the cross, but by his Resurrection.

This Resurrection presents connections with the mystery of the Incarnation. To whom must we attribute the Incarnation? It is the Son of God who, in Jesus, took on the flesh of the Virgin Mary: The Word of God then is, in Jesus, the final end of the Incarnation. On the other hand, in principle, we meet the Father for it is truly he, for all eternity, who begets the Son, who, in time, we came to call Jesus. Between these two terms is the power of God that is common to the three divine Persons which realizes the mystery, a realization that we attribute to the Holy Spirit.

In the re-Creation of the world, the Father sends his Son. He is born of Mary, the Holy Spirit impregnated the Mother and realized the union of the two natures in the Person of the Son. Saint Thomas sees the Resurrection in the same way. By appropriation, the Holy Spirit realized the Resurrection of Christ through the divine power, the mystery by which the Father remains at the origin through the conception of the divine plan and sending of his Son. He is glorified in terms of the mystery of the redemption. Saint Paul wrote that Christ had been "declared to be Son of God with power according to the spirit of holiness by resurrection from the dead" (Rom 1:4), and that reveals the role of the Holy Spirit in the glorification of Jesus to us: *If Christ ascended to heaven, it was through his own power; first of all, by divine power; secondly, by the power of the glorified soul which moves the body as it wishes* (S.T. IIIa, Q57:3 RD). The last excerpt of this text opens certain perspectives about a dogma that is too little known by Christians: we easily admit that Christ lifted himself to heaven through divine power, but the concept that *the glorified soul moves the body as it wishes* surprises us, explains the apparitions of the resurrected Lord, and is a part of our faith.

Easter is the celebration of Christ's Resurrection, the triumph of the Father who raised his Son who was put to death through the sins of man, the ultimate victory of the divinity of Jesus over his ravished humanity, and also the model and premise for our own resurrection. Perhaps it is on the last part of this phrase that I stumble the most. It is true that Christ was raised from the dead, but me? Yet:

"I believe in the resurrection of the body."

REFLECTION QUESTIONS

Do I see my one goal in life as to be living forever with God in heaven? Do I see that through Jesus Christ's Incarnation and Resurrection that this is possible? Now that I am aware that Jesus has sanctified all that is human (including death) by becoming flesh, do I approach my daily routine any differently? Do I seek God in all things, in every corner of my life, because I know that Jesus is present and alive in everything?

DAY TWELVE

The Ascension—Glorification

FOCUS POINT

Jesus Christ is humiliated twice and glorified twice. In his first humiliation, Jesus Christ became incarnate, taking on the flesh of lowly man. His resurrection from the dead glorified this first humiliation. In his second humiliation, Jesus Christ descended into hell to claim the souls—Adam and Eve and their descendants—previously conquered by death. Jesus Christ was glorified a second time following this humiliation, taking his rightful place at the right hand of his Father in heaven.

> *"He ascended into heaven*
> *and is seated at the right hand of the Father" (Credo).*

L et us not seek to imagine or give ourselves a representation of Jesus Christ's ascension and his glorification at the right hand of the Father; we would be led to ask ourselves the question, "and then what?" as if Christ, having left the earth's gravity, traveled beyond the solar system and galaxies. That is a false path, and one would reach an impasse! It was the risen Christ that the apostles saw ascending, a glorious Christ whose vision of glory would have blinded them if it hadn't been temporarily veiled at the moment of the apparitions. Paradoxically, it is when Jesus veils his glory that Jesus becomes visible (except perhaps at the Transfiguration) and when he disappears, it is in order to allow all of his glory to show through. The cloud in which the vision of the apostles lost themselves constituted the retreat of the veil, the full outpouring of the glorification, the sitting at the right hand of the Father. This is a mystery that is unfathomable to our carnal eyes but one which is offered to the eyes of our spirit.

Saint Thomas used the word "reward": *According to the Apostle, the exaltation of Christ was the reward for his humiliation. It follows from there that to his double humiliation there would be a double exaltation*" (C., 240, 1). The translation of the Latin *"praemium"* by "reward" brings a "scholarly" overtone into play and thus another of "justice," which is also unsuitable. The infinite love of the Father welcomed the Son, carrier of the sin of the world, through repentance for the world, according to the parable of the Prodigal Son (See Lk 15). That is the thinking of the Angelic Doctor since it sets up a double glorification in exchange for a double humiliation.

The hymn to the Philippians (2:5–11) celebrates the double kenosis, or abasement of the Word of God.

The first of these abasements aims essentially at the Word of God in his divine nature by coming into our world and assuming flesh. Saint Thomas only envisaged the abasements of Jesus, the Word of God incarnate, in his human life. The first abasement that was essential to the Incarnation was followed by another that Saint Thomas considered under two aspects: *"He was first*

*humiliated by suffering the night in a passible flesh that he had
assumed, then, when it was time, his body was deposited in a
tomb and his soul descended to hell"* (C., 240, 2). To these two
abasements, he would contrast two exaltations, well in line with
the Paulist thought expressed by the phrase "therefore God also
highly exalted him" (Phil 2:9). The paschal mystery then, brings
with it the succession of two abasements followed by two exaltations that correspond mutually to each other: *"The exaltation of
the resurrection, in which he returns from death to immortal life,
responds to the first humiliation; the exaltation to the ascension
responds to the second humiliation"* (C., Ibid). The loss of the
human life is found to be compensation through his entrance into
eternal life, while the descent to hell is through the glorification.

Next, in this section, we must discuss the different meanings
of hell versus hells. The Latin phrase "ad inferos" requires us to
place it in the plural in English, "to the hells," which is not a
familiar usage in English and which is different in meaning from
the singular "to hell." In our era, hell describes a place of dwelling for the damned, the nonsalvageable and, consequently, those
who have no hope. On the other hand, "the hells" describes a
place of waiting and hope for the righteous of the Old Testament.
It was there that Christ went in his descent, and from there, he
arose again to go to remove Adam and Eve (and their descendants) just as the icons of the Resurrection show.

Saint Thomas has a realistic view of things and of the humanity of Christ. Jesus' death, attested to by the nails and the wound
of the sword, arises from human ferocity; in the same way, the
resurrection will be "tested" by the invitation to place a finger on
the marks left by the nails and a hand on the wound in the side in
order to recognize: "My Lord and my God." In the same way, the
descent to the "hells" and the glorification aim at Christ's humanity: it is truly a cadaver of which we speak (even one united
to the divinity of Christ) that was placed in the tomb, rapidly
embalmed; it was the same body, resurrected, given life, and glorified that would seat itself at the right hand of the Father. Tho-

mas underlines this identity, already shown by Saint Paul, when he cites: *"He who descended is the same one who ascended far above all the heavens"* (Eph 4:10). What respect it imposes for a body that was torn, bruised, and twisted through suffering and death!

The Incarnation and Resurrection lead us to envisage the Word of God as coming amongst us, establishing his dwelling there, then rejected until a time when, glorified, it once again finds his place of origin. The meaning of faith apprises us of an anthropomorphic vision of the mystery: the Word of God leaving heaven temporarily. Saint Thomas underlines the immutability of God: *"According to the divine nature, he never left heaven, finding himself always and everywhere; from which, in Saint John he said: 'No one has ascended into heaven except the one who descended from heaven, the Son of Man'"* (Jn 3:13) (*Compendium* 240:2). The temporal and fleeting present of the descent from and ascent to heaven through the conception and death of Christ in his human nature is contrasted to the eternal Present of the Son of God in heaven in his divine nature. Becoming a man, the Word still remained God, his earthly presence did nothing to modify his divine omnipresence. The temptation of deception could assail us: where is the humanity of God if the Incarnation of the Word touches him in no way? Let us turn the phrase around: where would the divinity of God be if some act, no matter how great or important it may be, would change it? It is not a contradiction, but the mystery of the infinite in which nothing changes. Jesus went successively to Bethlehem, Nazareth, and Jerusalem, but being God, he transcends both time and place.

Saint Thomas attributes Jesus' own ascension to himself: *"Only Christ, of his own strength, ascended to heaven"* (C., 240, 3). Probably he was voicing his own thoughts here, but not entirely. Is he thinking of the Assumption of the Blessed Virgin Mary when he writes: *"The others couldn't ascend there by themselves, but through the virtue of Christ, having become parts of him (his body)"*? Or is he envisaging the general glorification of all Christians of which Mary's is a prototype? His essential view is the difference between the Ascension and the Assumption, to ascend by oneself or to be elevated by someone else. We would be tempted to assimilate the Ascension with the Resurrection, to attribute its effectiveness to the divine common all-powerfulness of the three divine Persons, and to "attribute" that to the Father as if he was the source of this powerfulness, in effect, would be to unite the Paulist idea of "reward" (already seen above) with all rewards that one has received from another. We could also "attribute" this Ascension to the Holy Spirit, the Source and Giver of all life, the Paraclete or "consoler," agent of all sanctification in grace and glory. Such does not seem to be the thinking of Saint Thomas; it seems to be that after the Resurrection, the humanity of Christ came back to life, already glorified. What it couldn't do for itself for the Resurrection, it could for the Ascension. The glorified soul of Christ had all the power over his body which was also glorious.

This first glorification is followed by another, the reward for the second humiliation, or descent into the hells, which is the sitting at the right hand of the Father. Saint Thomas warns us against all anthropomorphism: *"There is neither a right hand or a corporal sitting. But just like the right side is a place of honor for man, one wants it to be made understood that the Son is equal to the Father, having lost nothing in his divine nature but finding himself to be in perfect equality with him"* (C., 240, 3). Let us get rid of the image of an eternal throne. Jesus ascended to heaven corporally: "touch my hand...my feet." The problem is, then, one of the glorification of the body, sufficiently "real" to be touched and sufficiently subtle to be out of place. Relatively easily, we can accept the idea that the Son remained equal to the Father in spite of his Incarnation, but that of the glorification of his humanity fails us. It also fell short for the apostles before us, even though we could say that they had been witnesses to the glorious body.

There remains an example for us upon which we can reflect:

that of Mary. We could deny certain apparitions but not all of them. Did those who saw these visions see the body of Mary or an image of this body? That is another problem that we will leave to the specialists. What is important to us is that Mary, elevated to heaven in body and soul, is in a constant relationship with whoever prays to her, no matter when or from where these prayers may come, and at times she gives witness to certain privileged persons to the authenticity of her glorious body. My relationship with Mary is truly real. By giving his Mother to John: "Here is your mother," it is to all believers in general, and to me in particular that Jesus gives her. Let us not try to materialize to excess a spiritual reality, but let us not get rid of the glorification of the flesh either.

Jesus is seated at the right hand of the Father. Saint Thomas distinguishes the two natures in Jesus: *"According to his divine nature, the Son is in the Father in a unity of being with whom he shares the seat of royalty, that is, of power.... The Son of God, even according to his human nature, he is seated at the right hand of the Father, just like being elevated above all creatures in the dignity of the heavenly kingdom"* (C., 240, 4). The Angelic Doctor implicitly refutes all "subordination" which could come from the expression: *"seated at the right hand of the Father."* Christ is God, the Word of God, and in God all honor and glory comes back equally to the three divine Persons. This being well affirmed, the Word became flesh and was invited to "sit at the right hand of the Father." Thomas explains the expression by a comparison of a king to his assistants: *"whosoever participates in something through royal power is the strongest, and the king puts him on his right hand"* (C., 240, 4). In his glorification, the humanity created by Jesus is seen from the angle of his effective contribution to the work of redemption. It is by that work that the Word saved humanity, took on the sins of the world, and was nailed to the cross. Like the Incarnation did not prevent the Word from being God, the seating at the right hand of the Father also agrees with the reign of the Word jointly with the Father and the Holy Spirit.

The Ascension is a mystery of hope, Christ is the firstborn from the dead and glorified. His ascension offers living hope to humanity of a glorious and eternal life. Confirmed by the Assumption of Mary, this hope could not remain in vain. Christianity, far from being a disincarnated religion where the spirit completely challenges man entirely; the sacraments of Christian life remind us of this reality, the Ascension makes us see the destiny to which God calls us.

REFLECTION QUESTIONS

In what areas of my life would I like to be more humble? Do I tend to "put on airs" when I am with certain people? How can I change my approach to these people so they may see the humility and service of Christ within me? In what ways do I "anthropo-morphize" God? Could broadening or narrowing this perception aid me in my prayer life? Might I read other spiritual writers to gain an understanding of the way they perceived God during their life?

DAY THIRTEEN

The Blood of Christ

FOCUS POINT

The New Covenant between man and God is sealed with blood, the blood of Jesus Christ, the Lamb of God. Unlike the "blood seal" of previous covenants, this seal cannot be broken by man's sin. Because of Jesus Christ's life, death, and resurrection, man and God are united forever, and the blood of the God-Man has sealed it. There are no obstacles that can keep God and man apart under the New Covenant; God has opened the gates of heaven to his creation by shedding his very blood for our salvation.

"Listen; your brother's blood is crying out to me from the ground!" (Gen 4:10)

Saint Thomas's devotion to the Blessed Sacrament doesn't have to be established. The Office that he composed on the occasion of the institution of this feast is the most beautiful expression of his love. We stop here primarily at his "Spiritual Readings" concerning the Blood of Christ.

The Bible teaches us about the value of the blood that was shed as the Law prescribed it, in order to satisfy God and reconcile with him. If the blood of an animal is sufficient for the purification of sin and the reentry into grace with God, how much the Blood of Christ, the Lamb without stain, immolated on the wood of the cross, blood shed and spread for a multitude of sinners, could not be even more precious?

In the Eucharist, we receive this holy beverage. Saint Thomas underlines that it is: *"blood of virginal origin, since the wine of honor, the product of the flower of the vine, is the precious blood of Jesus Christ, who was born of a virgin"* (S.R., Part 7, 1); and the Blood of Christ never knew the corruption of sin. This blood is not only contained in the cup where the wine is transformed into the Blood of Christ, but it is also contained in the consecrated Bread. It is the total body of Christ that we receive: Body, Blood, soul, and divinity.

Through his death and resurrection, Christ defeated Satan, the prince of death. Washed in the blood of the Lamb, the Innocent, the Righteous, we are saved and reconciled with God; that is why Saint Paul said that we are "God's beloved children and called saints" (See Rom 8). Jesus died for the remission of our sins, our sanctification, so that all people living in this world would become like him, in his image: holy and immaculate.

Each Sunday (or each day), when we take communion with the Body and Blood of Christ, we share the Bread that was broken and drink from the cup of the Lord, from which comes this strength, this power of redemption that it contains and in which we believe. Saint Thomas, by referring to three texts, from Jeremiah, the Letter to the Hebrews, and the Acts, shows the holiness of the Blood of Christ.

"The Lord said: 'I made the whole house of Israel cling to myself,' that is, I united myself, in an inseparable way, with the complete human nature, the soul, the body, and the blood" (S.R., 7, 1).

Jeremiah (13:11) states: "For as the loincloth clings to one's loins, so I made the whole house of Israel and the whole house of Judah cling to me, says the Lord, in order that they might be for me a people, a name, a praise, and a glory. But they would not listen."

This is the theme of the Covenant that Saint Thomas comments on briefly. All people are called to be the fame, praise, and glory of God. God's desire is for all creatures to cling to him; his creations are nothing without their creator! It is, then, necessary for man, because of original sin, to be in perpetual movement towards his God. We know this, we are beings with "stiff necks" and God in his great mercy has had many covenants with us. But the new and eternal Covenant is God who became man. The Word united himself *"in an inseparable way, with the complete human nature, the soul, the body, and the blood"* (S.R., 7, 1). The Word of God became flesh and changed the human condition in all ways except that in which man drags, like a ball and chain, the sin that keeps him from totally clinging to his Creator. Yet if sin is not vanquished, human nature will remain separated from God: the union is not perfect. Let us note the terms *"in an inseparable way"* which signifies that this Covenant is definitive and indefectible. Christian marriage is a consequence of this "inseparable way," that is, the two spouses are united by God forever, forming one single body. "This is a great mystery and I am applying it to Christ and the Church" (Eph 5:32), since it is through this gift of his own blood that Christ becomes the Bridegroom of the Church.

Thomas continues: *"The Son of God, wanting to obtain salvation for mankind, endowed with flesh and blood, took the flesh and the blood of mankind, united them to himself, and elevated them to such a degree that we could truly say that it is the flesh and blood of a God"* (S.R., 7, 1).

Jesus, by adopting our nature, became like us, beings of flesh and blood. However, it is said that this blood and this flesh *"[were] united to him and elevated."* In effect, by taking on the human condition, he is also of a divine nature, without the shadow of sin which leads to death and that is how he elevated all of humanity, for his union with God remains total. The person living in the slavery of sin is dragged, under the devices of the devil, to a separation from God. The Blood of Christ, abundantly shed on the cross, was shed at an inestimable price, for it is by this blood that Jesus reduced Satan to nothing, thus obtaining the redemption of the world and the reconciliation with the Father. This great good found again opens the door for us to the kingdom of heaven, there, where eternal life dwells. That is what comes from the text that Thomas refers to: "Since, therefore, the children share flesh and blood, he himself likewise shared the same things, so that through death he might destroy the one who has the power of death, that is, the devil, and free those who all their lives were held in slavery by the fear of death" (Heb 2:14–15).

This inestimable value of the Blood of Christ that was shed in abundance, even when a single drop would have been sufficient for the redemption of the world, is proof of a great love. "There are three that testify: the Spirit and the water and the blood, and these three agree" (1 Jn 5:7–8)

By reporting the episode in Saint John where the soldier pierced Jesus' side through completely, Thomas made these comments: *"It is not said that the soldier injured Jesus' side, but that he opened it, in order to widen, in a way, the door of life ; it is from there that the Sacraments of the Church came, without which we could not go to* (eternal) *life"* (S.R., 7, 1).

It is also necessary for us to preserve this precious good that has been obtained for us through the blood of Jesus; for this, vigilance is important. It is to the pastors who are put at the head of the flock of the children of God that the responsibility goes, and Saint Thomas cites Saint Paul on this subject: "Keep watch over yourselves and over all the flock, of which the Holy Spirit has made you overseers, to shepherd the church of God that he obtained with the blood of his own Son" (Acts 20:28).

It is by the precious blood of Jesus, taken from his side, that the Church was born. It is by Christ, the head of the Church, of which we are its parts that life has been given to us; also, the sacraments of the Church are the source of life, the door to the kingdom.

"Whoever eats my flesh and drinks my blood will have eternal life." Why is the Eucharist represented under two aspects: bread and wine? To this question, Thomas gave the following answer: *"It was to show that he took on human nature in its entirety, and that he also completely, and at the same time, redeemed it, that is the body and the soul. For the bread refers to the flesh for it nourishes it; the wine to the soul because the wine produces the blood which is the seat of the soul, according to the physicians. That is why, if the sacrament was only received under one aspect, that would signify that it would only be effective to cause redemption in one of them, that is, the body or the soul, and no longer the two at the same time"* (S.R., 3). By the bread that signifies the body and the wine the soul, received from the Holy Sacrament of the Altar, the soul and the body are simultaneously restored for, in either the earthly or eternal life, the soul cannot be separated from the body.

The Eucharist is a *"royal banquet,"* to which the righteous and the sinners are called, in as much as, nothing is missing in the feast. It is a "royal banquet" for, by his death and resurrection, Jesus became Christ the King, the king of the living, that is, the king of the life of the body and the soul for eternity next to God, his Father.

The Bible is filled with descriptions of such sumptuous meals: *"'...this cup is the new covenant in my blood. Do this, as often as you drink it, in remembrance of me' (1 Cor 11:25), that is, you drink my blood in memory of my passion. For the passion of Jesus Christ comes back to one's memory in a more expressive manner by the consideration of the blood than by that of the body"* (S.R., 7, 3).

When Israel was delivered from slavery in Egypt, the blood of the immolated lamb without sin had been placed on the lintels and uprights of the doors; that was the sign for God to not knock at these houses. This blood rite is perpetuated with the Israelis who remember, each year, this deliverance by blood. Jesus is the Immolated Lamb of God, without sin and *"thus, the blood of Jesus Christ is the very memorial and expression of his Passion"* (S.R., 3). Who, amongst us hasn't seen an injured person bleed? For a long time afterwards, we are left with that mental image, "expressed" by the image of the blood flowing from the wound. Our memory of the body of the wounded person only takes second place for it is connected to the blood that expresses its suffering.

Christians receive the blood of Christ under the aspect of wine less often than in comparison to priests. For that, Thomas saw three reasons: the first was that the priest was the holy vase consecrated in a special manner; the second was to avoid spilling the precious blood because of the crowds that gather around the altar. *"In the desert, they had distributed bread to the crowd without a beverage. In the Last Supper, the Lord gave, to his apostles, who were few in number, and because they were his priests, not only his body under the aspect of bread, but also his blood under the aspect of wine* (S.R., 7, 3). The third reason is that of avoiding the error of believing that the body would be only in one aspect when it is in both.

The Blood of Christ is, through transubstantiation, under the aspect of consecrated wine, and his body in the same way under the aspect of bread; in both cases, his body is there by annexation. It is thus: as the priest sacramentally receives the Blood of Christ, the faithful also receive sacramentally, under the aspect of bread, the total Body of Christ.

The shedding of Christ's blood is for our sanctification and from the very time that we receive the total Body of Christ, our intelligence is called to recognize the virtue of the Blood of Christ for humanity. The grace that we receive *"is compared to God's paradise and the blood of Jesus Christ, spiritually spread into the soul, produced there, like in God's paradise, flowers of virtues of different colors; they are the roses of charity, the lilies of chastity, the violets of humility*" (S.R., Part 7, 5).

Saint Augustine said: "Where there is humility, you will find charity." Thus, then if our soul is strewn with the grace of the violets of humility, it also is strewn with the roses of charity. With respect to the lilies of chastity, they are a particular grace that is granted to some and given concrete form in consecrated celibacy.

For the greatest number, it will be the virtues of charity and humility that will be offered and these are essential to all Christian lives. In effect, "Blessed are the poor in spirit, for theirs is the kingdom of heaven" (Mt 5:3). This "God's paradise," received in this earthly life through the sacrament of the Eucharist, should permit a transformation, through our acts of love, of the fallow garden of those who have not yet had the spiritual joy of tasting the Body of Christ.

Christ gave us his body and his blood four times:

> *"By being born, he became our companion,*
> *at the table, our nourishment,*
> *on the cross, our ransom,*
> *by reigning, he gave himself in compensation"*
> (Feast of the Blessed Sacrament, Hymn of Praise).

REFLECTION QUESTIONS

Do I forgive easily? Do I have a harder time forgiving myself or others? What are the models of forgiveness in my life? Specific family members, friends, holy leaders? Am I aware that God's mercy is so great that there is nothing so bad that I have done that he will not forgive it if I seek his forgiveness? Do I attend to the sacrament of reconciliation regularly? If not, what is preventing me and how can I deal with this obstacle? Might there be a spiritual friend with whom I could discuss some difficulty I may be having?

DAY FOURTEEN

The Church, the Body or Bride of Christ

FOCUS POINT

Christ and the Church are united by love. Christ is the Head of the Mystical Body, the Church, and it is through the Head that the Body receives the graces that come from God the Father. All good things come to the Bride, the Church, through the loving Bridegroom, Jesus Christ. Our participation in the divine life of the present and the eternal heaven to come, comes from Christ and enters us by means of his Incarnation, the complete unity of God and man. This marriage between Christ and his Church is cause for great joy.

"*He is the image of the invisible God.... He is the head of the body, the church*" *(Col 1:15, 18).*

"*Where there is one body, there must be one head. By anal-*

ogy, we may call a multitude ordained to one end, with distinct acts and duties, one body. But it is clear that both men and angels are called to the same end, which is the glory of the divine fruition, the vision of God. Hence, the mystical body of the Church consists not only of men, but of angels. Now, of this multitude, Christ is the head, since he is nearer God, and shares his gifts more fully, not only than man, but even than angels; and both men and angels benefit from his influence since it is written (Eph 1:20–23): 'God put this power to work in Christ...and seated him at his right hand...far above all rule and authority and power and dominion, and above every name that is named, not only in this age but also in the age to come. And he had put all things under his feet and has made him the head over all things for the Church, which is his body, the fullness of him who fills all in all.' Therefore, Christ is not only the head of men, but also of angels" (S.T. IIIa, Q8:4 RD).

B efore meditating on this text of Saint Thomas, let us allow ourselves to be seized by the Holy Spirit:

- Men and angels are both called to the same end: the vision of God.

- In the diversity of our acts and duties, we are all called to be members in the same body.

Although "incarnate" when it offers its sacraments to men where water, bread, wine, and oil are indispensable, the Church reveals itself also to be very spiritual since it includes "the separated creatures" (from all bodies, according to Saint Thomas) that we call angels.

A same flow of graces, coming from the Father, passes through the Son, and is spread across and gives life to the entirety of the

Mystical Body, in order to reach "the full stature of Christ" (Eph 4:13).

The term "Bride of Christ," given to the Church, does not include Christ himself; it places the Church in a face to face with respect to him. The distinction between the persons, that of Christ and that of the Church, is affirmed thus through the loving connection that unites them. No matter how intense the latter is, it cannot "dissolve" but only "unite" people: the Church is never totally identified with Christ.

And yet we speak of it as the "Body of Christ," his total or Mystical Body, of which he is the head. The image tends to make people indistinct to the benefit of one entity: Christ-Church, one body given life by one soul, one life. The only distinction, if the word is still valid, establishes Christ as the head of the Body, and the Church as the totality of its members. *Just as the whole Church is called one mystical Body because of its likeness to the human body, whose diverse members perform diverse acts as Saint Paul teaches (See Rom 12:4 and 1 Cor 12:12), so likewise Christ is called the head of the Church because of a likeness to the human head"* (S.T. IIIa, Q8:1 RD).

Here, the duality has apparently disappeared, Christ and the Church are one. The distinction between the body and the head only concerns the parts of a single unique entity. Just like the head plays a pivotal role in the human body, it is the same for Christ and the Mystical Body: *"On account of his nearness to God, his grace is the highest and the first, though not temporally, since all have received grace on account of his grace"* (Ibid).

Christ had been established by the Father as being above all other living creations in time and space. Based on the fourth gospel, "We have seen his glory...full of grace and truth" (Jn 1:14), Saint Thomas describes that the bounty of Christ's grace, the life-giving flow from the Father and through him, Christ, was spread into the entire Body. This plenitude is relative to his mission as the universal "Redeemer" and even "Protector," for Christ could protect those whom he could not redeem. It is thus for the angels and for our humanity, represented by the Blessed Virgin Mary. From the continuation of the gospel text: "From his fullness we have all received, grace upon grace" (Jn 1:16), Saint Thomas concludes that the expression "Christ, the head of the Church" is found to be justified. It shows our deification or participation in the divine nature, as well as the same life that flows in Christ and in us.

Let us come back to our original text: *the mystical body of the Church consists not only of men, but of angels.*" Human pettiness and the strictness of man's spirit do not make him inclined to include angels in his church. Angels are not "redeemed" by Christ; the Word of God became man and not an angel, he did not die and rise from the dead for them! This restrictive viewpoint brings its own fruit—and great damage. Suppress the angels and the Church will be limited to our very restrained earthly horizons. That is not the Church of Christ that was designed by the Doctor of the Nations and the Angelic Doctor. Saint Thomas read that "he (Christ) is the head of every ruler and authority" (Col 2:10), and included them in his ecclesiastical vision, giving them a reason for it: *both men and angels are called to the same end, which is the glory of the divine fruition, the vision of God.*" Thomas didn't have the theological lyricism of the Greek Fathers, nor that of an Eric Peterson or Virgil Gheorghiu, so it is up to us to read between the lines: the meaning of life for the angels and for man is the same: reach the same contemplation of God, the same adoration and the unique Sanctus that allows us to catch a glimpse of what is in chapter six of the Book of Isaiah and the Book of Revelation.

Just as their natures differ, the paths of angels and men do. Through a unique act, the angel is introduced into the "Ecclesia," finds its place there, and participates in common adoration. Man must work for a long time to merit (if we could call it that), through a process that is more or less long, his reward for his efforts and searches, and he is often confronted with the traps of the Evil One. Man is essentially a "viator," always in motion, before being a "comprehender," pleased with his vision of God.

The liturgy depends on whoever officiates. *"Devotion given to God by man carries a double format: interior and exterior. Because man is made up of a body and a soul, both must give glory to God"* (S.T. Ia–IIa, Q101:2 RD). There must, then, be a special devotion that is rendered to God by the angels and another by man. Sacramental devotion is made for man. The angels' spiritual devotion encompasses that of the saints and surely our own in its spiritual aspect. Man is uncomfortable in thinking of "a Divine Heavenly Liturgy," that of the immolated and glorified Lamb, sung by the wise elders of the Old and New Covenants, celebrated by the Seraphim and the Cherubim, repeated in the hearts of the martyrs, virgins, and all the saints. A "western" vision, such as that suggested by the Van Eyck reredos in Gand, calls its complement "oriental" drawn from the icons of fire by bringing archangels into the picture, the ascetic fathers of the desert or the liturgists of the great basilicas. *"Angels are not beings that are 'in the process of advancing,' but beings that are "in possession" in that they can no longer either merit or grow in blessings"* (S.T. IIIa, Q62:9). The expression "triumphant Church" has not enjoyed a good reputation. Applied to our earthly time, it only evokes memories from which we can't draw joy; when applied to the heavenly Church, it is completely different. The immolated Lamb triumphs because, in him, life experienced death. The angels and archangels join together in adoration and thanksgiving, for their choice is a triumph of the grace of God over personal pride. Martyrs and confessors sing, in their act of thanksgiving, the triumph of the grace of Christ in them. Each angel and each man is called to the same essential glory of the vision of God, yet it is adjusted for each one according to his own destiny and earthly battle: "For those whom he foreknew he also predestined to be conformed to the image of his Son" (Rom 8:29).

Jesus said to Simon: "You are the rock and on this rock I will build my Church." Vatican II completed the ecclesiastical viewpoint of Vatican I: Saint Thomas would have approved of both. Heavenly, the Church is also earthly. Spread across all the world, it is universal; in time, it includes all the faithful, the believers in the Old and New Covenants. Faith is the criteria of inclusion: The Christian puts it in the Messiah who came and who will return, the Jew in the Messiah to come. Both express their beliefs through devotion: *"The Fathers of the Old Law, by observing the devotion to the Law, were carried to Christ by the same faith and love that carries us to him. That is why they belong to the same body of the Church as we do"* (S.T. IIIa, Q8:3). The progression of the Jewish faith to the Christian faith and to the glory of the saints brings along a progression from the mosaic liturgy to the Christian one and finally, to the heavenly one; the first foreshadows the second; both find their fruition in the last, that of the immolated Lamb. *"Amongst the gifts that God made to humans after the original fall, the first was that he gave his Son, 'For God so loved the world that he gave his only Son, so that everyone who believes in him may not perish but may have eternal life' (Jn 3:16). That is why the greatest sacrifice is the one by which Christ offered himself to God as 'a fragrant offering and sacrifice' (Eph 5:2). Because of that, all other sacrifices under the Old Law, having been offered like this unique sacrifice, foreshadow it just as the imperfect foreshadows the perfect. This is where this comment from the Apostle originates: 'Every priest stands day after day at his service, offering again and again the same sacrifices that can never take away sins. But when Christ had offered for all time a single sacrifice for our sins…' (Heb 10:11–12)…"* (S.T. Ia–IIae, Q102:3 RD). Thus, the three liturgies discover their unity in the paschal mystery of the death and resurrection of Christ.

Jesus said: "I am the light of the world." As the Bride of Christ, the Church must reflect the light of its transfigured Bridegroom on its face; as the Body of Christ, it receives, transmits, and diffuses this light. The prophet Isaiah cried: "Enlighten yourself, enlighten yourself Jerusalem." Saint Thomas highlighted six reasons for this transfiguration.

Since Christianity is a revealed religion, its doctrine constitutes an unequaled light that is projected on the mystery of God, man, and his salvation so that its ending has means to be reached. No other religion brings a light to bear on these fundamental problems, even if many participate in some particular points.

Given to everyone equally, this doctrine is received in a manner that is very unequal. Accessible to all, the kerygma reduces itself to the salvific formula: Jesus-Savior, but it can and must be deepened by each according to their natural abilities and gifts from God.

Grace, which is the participation in the divine and deifying nature illuminates the soul beyond that which all natural powers have the ability to do. The shadows of atheism reveal this light of faith which is grace.

The effect of the light, joy, transfigures the face of the Christian. We have criticized this absence of Christian joy, often forgetting that the joy of faith is something other than that of a happy temperament. Interior and supernatural, its external expression depends upon many circumstances that do not originate from it.

Saint Thomas writes that the eternal glory of the saints is extremely deep, it penetrates the being, is eternal, complete, and perfect. Each year, at the feast of All Saints, we celebrate this glory which our elders enjoyed. Just like our prayer lifts itself by them all the way to God, their intercession and joy re-descends upon us. The glory of the saints is that of "pilgrims." Just like the star led the wise men to the manger of God-made-man, the glory of the saints guides us and enlightens us on our journey.

Finally, the source of all light is found in God and in the Lamb. God is love; God is light. The Lamb has already enlightened the heavenly city to which, through faith, we belong.

> "In the end times, we will see what we have believed about God before. We will hold directly in our hands what we had hoped for distantly, it is there that I am 'seized' to (as Saint Paul speaks of it in Phil 3:12) 'press on to make it (the goal) my own.' This is not an engrossing egoism but the presence and desire to seize the goal" (C., 164).

REFLECTION QUESTIONS

How do I envision the relationship between myself and God? As a servant-master dynamic? As two close friends? As a marriage? As a body and its head? How does this understanding of God shape my attitudes toward others? Do I envision the relationship between God and the Church in a similar manner? Do I delight in the relationship I currently have with God? If not, to whom or to which sources can I turn for assistance? How does my understanding of my relationship with God affect my outlook on each new day?

DAY FIFTEEN

To See God!

FOCUS POINT

"Theological virtues lead man to perfect bliss," says Saint Thomas Aquinas. We strengthen our virtues as servants of God by adhering to the Ten Commandments. We also do well to hold strong to the two great commandments given to us by our Lord and Savior, Jesus Christ: Loving God with all that we are and loving our neighbor as we love ourselves. When we walk the path of God, and focus only on his will, we know his great love in our earthly life and move towards the eternal bliss of the "face to face" with him in heaven.

"Blessed are the pure in heart, for they will see God" (Mt 5:8).

To see God! Is that the height of wisdom or of foolishness? The height of pride or that of humility in the search? The desire could be for what is accessible, what is inaccessible leaves us indifferent, sad, or disappointed. But then why did God put in us the desire to see him if it would remain unfulfilled?

For Saint Thomas, it means that we must seize God, *"The ultimate and perfect blessing of man could only be in the vision of the divine Being"* (S.T. Ia–IIae, Q3:8 RD), seized in that which it distinguishes between the object that is God, the uncreated object of our blessing, and the very act of our seizing, which is a personal and individual act, a created one: *"The final goal of man is the uncreated good, God, who alone can fulfill the affection of man by his infinite love, but, from another angle, the final goal of man is something created in him that is nothing other than this seizing of God and the joy that flows from it"* (S.T. Ia–IIae, Q3:1 RD). Saint Thomas gives us the key to the enigma: *"A thing is perfect as long as it is in act: a possibility that never comes to its realization remains imperfect"* (S.T. Ia–IIae, Q3:2). God would have not put the desire into man's heart to see him if he hadn't foreseen the realization of this project. In that aspect, Saint Thomas agrees with Saint Augustine: *"That blessing is the sovereign perfection of man"* (Ibid).

A realist, Saint Thomas had strong doubts that all men embraced this ideal of dreaming of seeing God; each person conceives of happiness in his own way. Some people are happy with an artificial paradise that is obtained through alcohol or drugs, others aspire to a more humane life that is normal and benevolent. The harmony of sound or colors, for the musician or artist, creates an awakening of an immense desire. Philosophical or scientific research introduces the scientist into an intellectual paradise where knowledge is the ruler.

In Book Three of his *Summa Contra Gentiles*, Saint Thomas warns us about certain desires that could not bring about the happiness of man on earth: honors, glory, power, wealth, and pleasure. Sought in vain like the ultimate goal of all these desires, they are recaptured and reestablished in their legitimate place in eternal life which is the contemplation of God. Sought for themselves, these honors render man arrogant and ambitious, yet when they would be given to the servant of God, "we will also reign with him" (2 Tim 2:12). In the same way, it is preferable to wait for the glory of God rather than look for it too hard: "those who love your name exult in you, for you bless the righteous" (Ps 5:11–12). Wealth and power render man egoistic and unjust, but we will be given something better, all danger will be avoided: "...the righteous...he sets them forever, and they are exalted" (Job 36:7). Even the pleasure that comes from the desire of the senses will find perpetual enjoyment in our resting in the Lord because: "you will give them drink from the river of your delights" (Ps 36:8). Thus, the false bliss that man could seek on earth is not rejected by Saint Thomas; by rectifying it, he makes it have an aspect that is secondary, but real for true bliss. The dogma of the resurrection of the flesh, probably one of the most "forgotten," and that of "eternal life" leaves many Christians indifferent or feeling that they are dreaming. The first assures us of the realization of our fundamental desires (even if the means of this realization fails us), while the second places us directly before the importance of the bliss.

"Theological virtues lead man to perfect bliss" (S.T. Ia–IIae, Q62:3); faith, hope, and charity bring us to God, and permit us to reach the inaccessible and introduce the Almighty into our life and in our life in him. Just like the two other theological virtues, faith is a freely given gift from God; it enables us to know him, at least partially, for it is a free act—we believe because we want to believe—it clearly distinguishes itself from proof. Faith will always be an obscure light and the believer will be a "watcher of the dawn." We believe in the Word of God which comes from hearing it, not from seeing it. With an increase in listening to the Word comes the desire to see, a desire that finds its realization in bliss, "for we walk by faith, not by sight" (2 Cor 5:7). Faith, then, is only a first stage, reached by successive acts of faith, in

view of a goal. To progress is to already reach the goal, a real contract with him. Necessary to the intelligible, the sensory experience is a part of it; necessary on earth, faith already is a part, in a certain sense, of the blessed vision; Saint Thomas calls this an *"antecedent"* (S.T. Ia–IIae, Q3:3 RD). In imperfect bliss, sensory joy lifts the spirit, while in the perfect one, the bliss of the spirit is reflected back on the body (See S.T. Ia–IIae, Q3:3). We can conclude from this that faith opens more onto true bliss, perfect bliss, than on the imperfect for the joy of believing first invades the soul and the spirit so that it only reflects back afterwards on the body. By leading towards bliss, faith could not constitute a view of its own being. Faith is a belief in the semi-obscure, while bliss is the full vision of God.

Faith is a cause for hope. Just like we want good for a friend whom we love and those who love us want good things for us, it is the same with God, the Master of all good, in whom we put all of our hope. It aspires to the complete and perfect possession of eternal life that we already possess as a seed, since Christ said, "Those who eat my flesh and drink my blood have eternal life" (Jn 6:54) and, as well, "anyone who hears my word and believes him who sent me has eternal life" (Jn 5:24). Death is inevitable for those who want to enter into glory, but it is feared by man instinctively. Why this fear? With all of his being, man aspires to bliss but fears the loss of that which he possesses on earth and, even more, the loss of his affective attachments. This is proof that he has not yet reached the perfect love that necessitates him to know only God and everything in him. The gospel also tells us: "For now we see in a mirror dimly, but then we will see face to face. Now I know only in part; then I will know fully, even as I have been fully known" (1 Cor 13:12). A long purification is necessary.

In third place in the order of theological virtues, charity is really first, the essential one in the order of perfection; it leads the others and subsists only in the kingdom of heaven where we will live only of love and with love. Saint Thomas saw four objects of charity: *"Charity extends not only to the love of God but also to the love of neighbor"* (S.T., IIa–IIae, Q25:1 RD), since man must love himself, having been loved by God (See Ibid, 4) and even his own body: *"It doesn't come from a bad precept as the Manicheans said, but from God, and we can use it in the service of God...that is why we must love our own body with the same love by which we love God"* (Ibid, 5).

In the Old Covenant, the first and the greatest commandment had been "one must love the Lord our God with all our heart and all our soul," which is followed and immediately completed by the phrase "and love one's neighbor as oneself." The priority of the love of God goes without saying; that of the neighbor, taught at an early age, is often brought to mind as: "He who says that he loves God and doesn't love his neighbor is a liar."

In the New Covenant, Christ joins the two commandments into a single one: "Love one another as I have loved you" (Jn 13:34). He loved his Father by being obedient to him all the way to death.

Saint Paul tells us "the love of God enflames us," the fact shows us the difficulty met by this love. Can we love God with all of our strength? Totally? Because everything is united in him, we can't love just his goodness or his mercy at the expense of his justice, nor his transcendence at that of his immanence. There is not one spirituality that is exclusive of another; perhaps a priority, but not an exclusivity. *"Taken from the viewpoint of man, the word 'totally' signifies that man must love God with all of his strength and that everything in him must be ordered to this love of God according to what is written in Deuteronomy 6:5"* (S.T. IIa–IIae, Q27:5). Here, the Christian appears to be consecrated to God. Thérèse of Lisieux had understood this; she, who was gravely ill, "walked for a missionary"; to the extreme, the martyr loves God with all of his body, delivered to the torture rack or to the fire. *"No creature can love God infinitely, neither through natural love, nor infused; his love remains limited"* (Ibid). Perhaps the Holy Spirit loved God in us infinitely, but then "it was no longer I who saw, but Christ within me."

Charity for our neighbor, received from God with the Holy Spirit is not granted once and for all; it has its daily requirements: "love is patient; love is kind; love is not envious or boastful or arrogant or rude" (1 Cor 13:4–5). If it is true that we have instinctive charity within us like that which is seen in acts like helping an unknown injured person, it is also true that we have sin within us, inherent to our nature, which is an obstacle to the growth of charity all the way to even removing it completely.

"The perfect bliss that will come after death is an immediate vision of God, like that of a man who is right before us" (*Summa Contra Gentiles*, III, IL). A face-to-face meeting that makes us cross a threshold at the ultimate goal and then "when he appears to us, we will be like him and participants in his own bliss," for man can only reach that *"by the virtue of God and thanks to a sort of participation in the divinity"* (S.T. Ia–IIae, Q62:1).

> "My soul thirsts for God,
> for the living God.
> When shall I come and behold
> the face of God?" (Ps 42:2).

REFLECTION QUESTIONS

Am I aware of the Ten Commandments in my daily life? Do I contemplate the role they play in my life? Might I take some time to read what the Catechism has to say about the commandments and the subtleties they entail? Am I focused on the two great commandments that Jesus speaks of? In what ways do I seek to love the Lord with all that I am? How does this translate into love for myself and love for my neighbor? What does it mean to love others as God has loved me? How far can I take this (with God's grace) in my daily life?

Bibliography

Barron, Robert. *Thomas Aquinas: Spiritual Master*. Crossroad Publications, 1996.

Bunson, Matthew E. *The Angelic Doctor: The Life & World of Saint Thomas Aquinas*. Our Sunday Visitor, 1994.

Gallagher, David A., ed. *Thomas Aquinas & His Legacy*. Catholic University Press, 1994.

Gilson, Etienne H. *Wisdom & Love in Saint Thomas Aquinas*. Marquette Publications, 1951.

Jenkins, John I. *Knowledge & Faith in Thomas Aquinas*. Cambridge University Press, 1997.

Keenan, James F. *Goodness & Rightness in Thomas Aquinas's Summa Theologiae*. Georgetown University Press, 1992.

Kreeft, Peter, ed. *A Summa of the Summa: The Essential Philosophical Passages of Saint Thomas Aquinas's Summa Theologica Edited & Explained for Beginners*. Ignatius Press, 1990.

Maritain, Jacques. *Saint Thomas & the Problem of Evil*. Marquette Publications, 1942.

O'Meara, Thomas F. *Thomas Aquinas Theologian*. University of Notre Dame Press, 1997.

Pegues, R.P. *Catechism of the Summa Theologica of Saint Thomas Aquinas*. Roman Catholic Books, 1993.

Rogers, Eugene F., Jr. *Thomas Aquinas & Karl Barth: Sacred Doctrine & the Natural Knowledge of God*. University of Notre Dame Press, 1999.